D1349868

FULL SCORE

NEVILLE CARDUS

FULL SCORE

505979

CASSELL · LONDON

CASSELL & COMPANY LTD
35 *Red Lion Square, London, WC1*
Melbourne, Sydney, Toronto
Johannesburg, Auckland

© Sir Neville Cardus 1970
All rights reserved. No part of this publication
may be reproduced, stored in a retrieval system,
or transmitted, in any form or by any means,
electronic, mechanical, photocopying, recording
or otherwise, without the prior permission of
Cassell and Company Ltd.

First published 1970

I.S.B.N. 0 304 93643 X

HERTFORDSHIRE
COUNTY LIBRARY

5059279

B/CAR

Made and printed in Great Britain by
William Clowes & Sons, Limited, London and Beccles
F.570

To David Ascoli
who has conducted this book
and
maintained the right tempo

Contents

Manchester Guardian   1
    'Prentice Years   3
    Samuel Langford   10

Edwardian Music-Hall   25

Music-Makers   35
    Paderewski   37
    Arrau   40
    Rubinstein   48
    Schnabel   51
    Elena Gerhardt   58
    Menuhin   61

Milady   65

Vienna Memories   75
    Noch einmal Wien!   77
    Lotte Lehmann in Vienna   83

Green Thoughts in a Green Shade   95
    Cricket of Vintage   97
    C. B. Fry   116
    Arthur Mailey   120
    A Midsummer Day's Dream—and Awakening   125
    Absent from Leeds, 1929   129

More Music-Makers   135
    Klemperer   137
    Furtwängler   141
    Schwarzkopf, Fischer-Dieskau and Legge   145

Eroticism in England   153

Australian Years   161

Return of the Native   191

MANCHESTER GUARDIAN

'Prentice Years

It was my good luck to emerge from a youth of casual labour and self-education to a job on the *Manchester Guardian* in C. P. Scott's reign. He had little use for the specialist worker, the one-track mind. He expected his principal leader-writer to have the knowledge and skill to turn, at a pinch, to a first-night notice of a play, or a Hallé Concert. He used me as a reporter covering local government, outbreak of fire, and as reviewer of music-hall performances; so that in turn I coped with Manchester City Council Committees, law courts, George Robey, Beethoven, Sir Thomas Beecham, Gracie Fields, with an occasional Test match as a sort of side-line. It was in a notice of a music hall perform-ance at the Ardwick Empire that the reporters' room of the *Manchester Guardian* discovered Gracie Fields, then nationally unknown, playing in a sketch called 'Mr. Tower of London'. There was C. E. Montague to show us the light, not by word spoken (for he was a shy man) but by his writing. Thus:

'The critic proper is neither a tutor in the technics of the art which he criticises, nor an examiner commissioned to allot marks to its practitioners in accord with strict distributive justice, as in the sight of God. He, too, in his humble way, is an artist, as they are. And every artist's business is to express his own individual, autonomous, possibly uncommonly wayward sense of something that presents itself to him.'

'His own uncommonly wayward self'—here was the cue for action amongst the *Manchester Guardian* young men, Howard Spring, A. V. Cookman, Ivor Brown, Alan Dent, Harry

3

Boardman. In a week I would, apropos the B minor Mass, a
musical comedy or Jack Hobbs, give an account of the way I
enjoyed, or did not enjoy them. I have, only the other day, found
a cutting of a notice of Karsavina dancing at the Palace Theatre,
Manchester, written by the young reporter who was, inexplicably it seems to me now, myself:

'Karsavina comes at last to Manchester. There is no opera
house here for her, so we must be thankful that the music-
hall, our Palace of Varieties, risks now and then a little on
genius. She is, of course, not in her right setting; but her art
comes through triumphantly, for all that. Karsavina is good
enough to remind us of Pavlova'—[*would you believe it?*]—
'which is not to say she is at all like Pavlova.' [*I pause here, as
I quote, for a retake of breath.*] 'She has not Pavlova's mysterious
half-lights; Karsavina moves in a world of primary colours.
And how vividly her art does suggest them!—the adagio
from *Sylvia* last evening was a movement in soft blue; the
Oiseau d'Or a capriccio in flashing yellow. She sets the dramatic senses working at the same time, yet never forgets, even in
her purely descriptive moments, to *dance*, always to be splen-
didly rhythmic. So it would seem that dancing—which, if one
doesn't misquote Wagner, was the mother of music—has extended its scope, even in the same way as music itself:
"programme" and "absolute". In "programme" music the
melodic and harmonic material is selected and developed so
that it may be descriptive of some sort of literary or poetic
scheme: a sequence of events, with a central character, as in
Strauss's *Till Eulenspiegel*, or an atmosphere, as in Debussy's
"L'après-midi d'un Faune".' [*Here, you see, young Cardus was
instructing grandmother Ernest Newman the way to suck eggs. And
remember, he was writing a notice of Karsavina dancing in a Manchester music-hall.*] ' "Absolute music",' [*continued this remarkable notice, written 'on the night', after some, I suspect, preliminary
secret preparation*] 'on the other hand, is, as Mr. Arthur Symons
once put it,' [*I admire that 'once put it'*], 'content with beauty
and to be itself. It lives certainly in its own world, moving
along strictly musical lines; and the emotions and sensations

4

it expresses and evokes are hardly to be expressed and evoked by any other art, while they set a verbal analysis rather at defiance. These two classes of music may be represented by the Sultan motif in Rimsky-Korsakov's *Schéhérezade*, and by any phrase in Mozart's "Eine kleine Nachtmusik". The one can, of course, intrigue the ear simply as a sequence of musical sounds, but the significance is in its veracity to a definitely dramatic and pictorial idea which you need to have in mind before you can appreciate that veracity. The other has an *absolute* quality, a loveliness which will strike any ordinary musical intelligence at once, without the aid of exegis.' [*'Exegis'*, *mark you!*] 'And' [*Karsavina, wait for it!*] 'in dancing we have a similar broad classification. Maud Allen has given us "programme" dances as "psychological" and as compli-cated as a problem play; and unless we possessed the literary or dramatic key to her movements and gestures they were not particularly satisfying, so much did they surrender of the rhythmical beauty which we have a right to expect from dancing. And Genée has given us "absolute" dancing; for that matter, so on occasions has Miss Allen,' [*a charitable concession*] 'in which there has been a quite abstract beauty of line, mass and motion. Around these two sorts of dancing, schools have raised themselves contendingly, just as the "absolute" musicians tilt at the "programmists". But in both cases, antagonism is wrong-headed. The greatest composers have shown that the best qualities of "programme" and "absolute" music will combine. Wagner, in the "Forest Mur-murs" paints a scene and at the same time manages to charm the purely musical ear. So will a great dancer like Pavlova or Karsavina' [*I had not forgotten her, after all*] 'satisfy the rhyth-mic sense by sheer poetry of motion, yet all the time tell us a story, thus moving us with a dual appeal. Taglioni herself could hardly ever have captured the finest nuance of rhyth-mic play of bodily forces as Karsavina did in *L'Oiseau d'Or*; and it is certain she never stirred the pictorial and dramatic senses as Karsavina did here.' [*Taglioni dragged in for compari-son by a* 'Manchester Guardian' *reporter in 1920!*]

[*And now the crescendo, and curtain*]: 'In *L'Oiseau d'Or*,

5

Karsavina is a shimmering wonderful bird. With what a swift and throbbing play of gesture she suggests a proud spreading of feathers, and an amorous palpitating breast! And the adagio from *Sylvia* saw a different Karsavina, just as marvellous. Here the movement was grave and deliberate. Now and then a superb attitude was transfixed in a purely statuesque pose that passed in a flash to motion again. There was never a hint of routine technique in all this; no studied "effects", and no mere mimicry. The dancing seemed to be all got by a few fleeting improvisations. And it had gone from us almost before we knew it was there. . . .'

All of this was written, I guess, at the end of a day long occupied in a report of some Council meeting in the Manchester Town Hall, or an investigation into post-war food prices in the Shudehill Market. 'Karsavina at the Palace Theatre.' And the notice was written not on a typewriter, but by hand; as Oscar Wilde said, after carefully inspecting Frith's huge canvas called 'Derby Day',—'all done by hand, I suppose'. Bliss was it in that *Manchester Guardian* meridian for a young journalist to be alive, to have space to breathe as a writer, to have the company, deep down in the cellars of Manchester's cafés, of Langford, Howard Spring, Wadsworth (later a great 'M.G.' editor, but in those days, like myself, a day-by-day reporter). No University, Oxford, Cambridge, Harvard or any other, has given a growing impressionist mind and temperament an education so full, real, humane, as that given by the old 'M.G.'. But the natural receptivity had to be there, born within. Wadsworth and myself were, in war-time, at first discarded by the military Medical Board as physically 'not fit for active service'. We were temporarily relegated to 'C.3', a sort of waiting-list. Then came the 'comb-out'—vivid word, as though we of the temporarily 'rejected' were lice. Wadsworth and I were both passed as 'fit for garrison duty abroad'. We received a shilling, our first day's army pay, after the Medical Board had deemed us as young men likely to serve 'the Cause'. I reported that evening to C. P. Scott. I told him that Wadsworth and I had both been called up. He sat at his desk in his sanctum, bust of the blind Milton behind him. 'But,' he expostulated, 'I can't have my staff *denuded* in this way.' ('Denuded' was his word.) 'I can't have my staff denuded in this way. Montague enlisted the first day war broke out. I have lost Gordon Phillips, Spring and Cookman. I shall at once speak to Lloyd George. . . .' I gave him, at his request, the Medical Board's papers of instructions about our call-up. I heard no more of them, nor did Wadsworth. Our All-Father, Charles Prestwich Scott, certainly wasn't having the *Manchester Guardian* denuded to its peril. Round about this period, C.P.S. used me as his secretary during mornings (usual reporter duties from 12.30 p.m. onwards, same salary, roughly 30 shillings weekly, 1/6 for lunch, 1/- for tea). Lloyd George called one day at Scott's home at the Firs, Fallowfield, a highly social part of suburban Manchester. I showed the Prime Minister into Scott's study. After an hour or so, Lloyd George emerged and, as I led him to the door to his car, he turned to me saying, as though he had known me all his life: 'Cunning old rascal, Scott.' I was rather shaken; C.P.S. was our symbol of the Liberal Nonconformist conscience. When I went to see Scott, immediately on Lloyd George's departure from the house, Scott said to me: 'Lloyd George, you know, Cardus— an unscrupulous rogue.'

As I say, no specialist segregation, no priggish exclusiveness on the *Manchester Guardian*, least of all in the reporters' room, presided over by the elegant, witty Haslam Mills. Karsavina and 'absolute' and 'programme' music one night; next week I am sent to a musical comedy, *The Kiss Call*, and the embryonic Cardus produced a notice containing these late-night reflections:

'The piece itself is so typical of its kind that it might well be used as the basis of an examination-paper for aspiring critics of musical comedy. The following questions would need to be answered correctly to win a diploma:

1. Give reasons why you think the play is named *The Kiss Call*.

2. What happened to the plot for twenty minutes in Act II?

3. Deduce the time of the year of its setting from costumes worn by the ladies.

4. The music is by Ivan Caryll, with "additional numbers" by Arthur Wood. Give instances from the score demonstrating which is the music of which.

5. Why are "additional numbers" always needed in the making of a musical comedy? Do you think that the physical and mental strain of writing the full score of a musical comedy too great on the brain of one man?

6. Give instances of "additional numbers" in Mozart.

7. Amongst the "lyrics" of *The Kiss Call* the name Henrietta is made to rhyme with somebody "who met her". Do you think this is permissible? Give reasons, if any . . .'.

Nobody except a half-wit will conclude that I call back these early works from the obscure because of any vanity. They were written nearly sixty years ago, by a young man I can now look back upon as though he had been my son, and dead long ago. Besides, by remembering these journalistic spreadings of wings, I re-live his 'prentice years yet again, with envy of his burgeoning period on the greatest of newspapers, the most inspiring for those who worked for it. Alistair Cooke has written eloquently in praise of the *Guardian* of our present epoch, and has, while doing so, stated that the *Guardian* has rid itself of the old 'piety', obviously having in mind some notion of the moral and mental obsessions dominating the paper as it was daily presented under the benevolent dictatorship of Scott. The fact is that in my 'prentice years on the *Manchester Guardian*, the paper was a perpetual source of wit; the Montague metaphor, the Haslam Mills flashing vignette of Gracie Fields. There was, of course, high seriousness in the long leaders. Compared with the *Guardian* of today, the *Manchester Guardian* under Scott was often actually flippant. Every morning somebody would write a memorable sentence, stimulating the mind and also the nerve of risibility.

Books, nay literature, were composed from the day-by-day copy supplied to the *Manchester Guardian* from one and all, from Montague and from the most utilitarian shorthand collector of news in the most talented reporters' room ever to be gathered together in a daily newspaper.

Samuel Langford

'The last sonata of Beethoven offers surely the most striking illustration there is of that unity in seeming contrasts which is the secret of the highest genius. Here is nothing, apparently, but a grim contrast between the starkest tragedy and that calm and eternal faith which is its only healer. Somewhere, in the soul of this music's creator, those elements are reconciled and fused. He tells us little of the process, but only its results. The final variations approach so nearly to a mechanical perfection that the contemplation of its nearness almost brings a shudder to the mind. Yet where shall we find music more divinely separated from the mechanical than those first variations whose whole existence seems to be the blissful stirring of an inward life? The apotheosis of the shake, with which this sonata ends, and in which the whole mechanical construction and subtlety of this sonata finds its solution, may be likened to those studies of light with which Turner in his last years baffled his beholders. The comparison is not far-fetched, nor a comparison with the moving glass, the smoothest of all poetic rhythms, in which Dante turns his verse . . .'

This is a quotation from a music notice written 'on the night', by Samuel Langford, critic of the *Manchester Guardian* from 1906 to a few weeks before his death in 1926, when he had arrived at his sixty-fourth year. From 1919 I served under him as assistant music-critic and, in 1926, was subjected by C. P. Scott to the severe challenge of following in the succession to Langford,

Newman and Arthur Johnston—which was very much like expecting a cricketer to go in to bat after a long, consecutive and masterful exhibition of stroke-play by Hobbs, Bradman and Hammond. Langford was a man of ample though shortish build, with a wispy beard, or rather, I would call them, whiskers. He wore his clothes loosely, unbuttoned at important coverings of his anatomy. Yet at a Hallé Concert in Manchester, in Richter's period, he would appear transmogrified in evening dress. His face was a mingling of the faces of Brahms and Moussorgsky; he was, in fact, a marvellous admixture of scholar and peasant. His voice had, at times and in the appropriate place, the intonation and accent of a professor, a don; at others, suiting expression to company, he would emit, snuffle or chuckle out his conversation as though in the Mermaid Tavern with Falstaff, with whom occasionally he suggested kinship, just as, on other occasions, he might have had relationship with Goethe. He could comfortably have gone into the company of each. Falstaff or Goethe.

He was born in Withington in a timbered house, surrounded by a garden ablaze, in season, with flowers, mainly delphiniums. He was in fact a cultivator of flowers, with a stall in the market in Shudehill, Manchester. He couldn't make the stall pay its way, so at last he appointed a manager, somebody who, unlike Langford, knew at sight the difference between the credit and debit side of a ledger. I asked him, some months following the appointment of this manager, if the 'business' was financially improving. 'Yes', he replied, his blue eyes closing, as he added in a chortle, 'yes,—I owe nothing now, except borrowed money.' One winter day, as we walked together along Cross St., Manchester (he didn't walk, he shuffled), I noticed a tear in one of my gloves. 'Nice state of things', I said, 'for a member of the staff of the *Manchester Guardian*.' He replied with 'I've got more important garments in a worse condition'.

He went to Leipzig in his twenties to study piano and music generally, his teacher Carl Reinecke; but his stubby, short fingers stood in the way of a complete technical command of the keyboard. Nonetheless, I have heard no pianist who was Langford's equal playing the late Intermezzi of Brahms; he was, in these autumnal pieces, Brahms reincarnate. On his deathbed he said to me: 'If you write my obituary don't make too much of my music criticism. Say something about my flowers.' Something, too, he could have implored, to the point of his reading, which had a great range, notably taking in stride nearly all Elizabethan and Restoration literature; and German. He would quote Goethe anywhere, in a concert review, or on the top of a tram. All the editorial staff of the *Manchester Guardian*, in Langford's and my day, went to the office, and departed for home towards midnight, by tram. Nobody had a car, not even C. E. Montague, Sidebotham (Balliol aristocrat), Professor L. T. Hobhouse, the brilliant Harry Sacher. Only C. P. Scott journeyed home to office and back by personally owned transport—a bicycle. Langford would hold court in the last tram of the night, to Fallowfield—at the top of the double-decker hold court to the rest of us, colleagues or general nocturnal public. Sometimes the official collector would interpose to inspect tickets. Langford, of course, had mislaid his. But the ticket collector himself would join with us in search of the ticket, grovelling and saying: 'Quite all right, Mr. Langford. Don't let me interrupt you. We'll find it.' Meanwhile Langford would continue: 'These Scotts and Montagues, aye, fine nineteenth-century radicals, Montague a virtuoso writer. But they've no juice in them, no juice.' When it was pointed out to him that, between them, Scott and Montague had produced a numerous progeny, his retort was: 'Aye, and none of 'em conceived in joy.'

Apart from his few years in Leipzig, where, I am sure, he spent as much time talking in cafés as in company of Reinecke, he was self-educated. I have never been able to discover how he entered journalism. He had reached his fortieth year before he wrote for the *Manchester Guardian*; and this is the only newspaper he ever wrote for. His primary profession and love were, as I have indicated, floriculture. Herbert Sidebotham, first leader writer of the *Manchester Guardian*, under the eye and jurisdiction of C. P. Scott, took the risk of employing Langford as deputy music-critic to Ernest Newman, who round about 1905 was making his reputation, notably by informing the Manchester public one Friday morning that at last night's Hallé Concert it had been pretty obvious that Dr. Richter's acquaintance with the score of *Romeo and Juliet* of Berlioz was not exactly close or of long duration. Langford at first suffered severe labour-pain producing a music notice; but when I worked with him he covered page after page as naturally and easily as he talked. He would sit at his desk, back from a Hallé Concert at ten o'clock, and, in handwriting akin to Shakespeare's, his notice of 1200 words was ready for the composing room at eleven o'clock, or not much later. As he transmitted his thoughts to paper, using a lead pencil, he ate dates from a box, spitting the stones right and left, even to the room's remotest corners. Meanwhile, from his pencil was going down on to paper something like this:

'Rosenthal is probably the most rapid of living pianists, yet there is nothing of bluff or chance in his swiftest flights. He is the most sparkling and also the most deliberate of players. Amazingly animated in details on the whole, we yet found him once or twice guilty of comprehensive readings which diminished rather than enhanced the animation of the music. The drive down to the close of the scherzo in the sonata' [Chopin: B minor] 'was a case in point; and in the ascending passage of semi-quavers near the close of the final movement, where the composer's idea seems no more than an ornamented succession of chromatic major thirds, he sought out a likeness to the main theme of the movement which seemed far-fetched . . .'

Langford did not go to concerts armed with a suitcase of scores as today many music-critics in London do. They pore over them even if the *Figaro* Overture or the Fifth Symphony of Beethoven are undergoing performance. I once sat next to an esteemed colleague who rapidly followed the *Barber of Seville* Overture of Rossini by means of the score; at the crescendo he was turning over the leaves at so desperate a speed that I had to turn up my coat collar to avoid discomfort of the draught he provoked. I remember, though, that actually I once saw Langford engrossed in a score during the playing of a string quartet by some now obsolete academy professor. I spoke to him during the concert's interval. 'Never before seen you with a score at a concert, Sammy', I said. 'Ah', he replied, 'it was such a boring work that I was going over Beethoven's Op. 135.'

Seldom did he discuss music in technical terms beyond the comprehension of the average educated listener. 'Musicians sometimes need to talk technique', he would say, paraphrasing Wagner in a letter to Liszt, 'but the public should never hear of it.' In conversation his wit was pungent. Curiously, he rarely wrote for a laugh or even a smile in any of his music writings. He took musical, philosophical and poetic views of a composition, the three perfectly blended; and always he approached a work and an artist with respect. He was, as man and critic, at Ernest Newman's extreme. His knowledge and culture were second to none; he simply wore his erudition as comfortably as he wore his ample coat and trousers. I can recapture, even as I write these lines, half-a-century after I last went into his room to see him bent over his desk, the lamp-light endoming his great forehead, finishing an account of a Beethoven chamber concert, thus—(apropos the Quartet in A minor, Op. 132):

'If these beauties were born of human weakness and frailty, and have come from the hardness of physical crisis, as the slow movement of thanksgiving for the recovery from sickness in the closing quartet so touchingly depicts, then there is something to be said even for weakness and sickness as an inspiration in the arts. And when with that weakness goes such gigantic spiritual strength as the overtowering attempts of these last quartets show, then we may regard with solemn pride the human nature which is capable of such efforts in such extremes. It is something to belong to the same race of beings as Beethoven.'

Having writ (the only word for it) this closing sentence, he would pick up the sheaf of his 'copy', hand it next door to his sub-editor (sometimes the sub-editor was myself), not looking through the pages, not always numbering them. Then he would say, 'Come for a nightcap in the "Thatched House"', and stumble down the office stairs. Most likely his mind had by now modulated to Manchester City's chances next Saturday, or if a cricket rubber in Australia were in progress, he mumbled his views about Gregory, and fast bowling from Spofforth onward.

I was drawn to him, not only because of his ample nature and broad accommodating mind, but by his distrust of formal academic education. As a boy he had planted flowers, and his hands were perpetually in the soil of a garden. Myself, as a boy, pushed a handcart around Manchester, sold chocolates in Miss Horniman's Gaiety Theatre, and also had early come to love flowers if only by selling them at Easter outside an inn in Northenden, Cheshire. He never spoke to me pedagogically, never consciously instructed me; he simply talked, usually deep down in basement cafés on foggy days in Manchester. Langford was fond of saying that all good writing, and good living, were discursive. When I began to write cricket reports for the *Manchester Guardian,* I followed the conventional press box procedure; I made notes of the number of fours a batsman hit, the time he stayed at the wicket, the amount of overs bowled in a given period, and so on. One day, at Old Trafford, Langford saw me writing down this factual data. 'Throw your notebook away', he said, 'watch the players and get the hang of their characters.' He didn't quite set me on the right track, but gave me the encouraging push. He insisted that I should read Goethe, and when I let him know that I was ignorant of the German language and added 'I'd better arrange for some lessons', he brushed the idea to the winds: 'No; read *Faust* with a dictionary.'

Under C. P. Scott, *Manchester Guardian* men, leader-writers or reporters, were expected to turn their attention to all manner of jobs. Scott was not satisfied by the one-track specialist. Herbert Sidebotham, brilliant with a first leader, long in length, three paragraphs—exposition, development and recapitulation— wrote about the first performance of *Der Rosenkavalier* in Manchester; he was a good musician. A. V. Cookman, usually coping with trouble in Ireland or the threats of a National Strike, was sent by Montague as deputy dramatic critic to discuss Shaw or J. M. Synge. Howard Spring, swift with Pitman's shorthand, would be expected to cover events ranging from a speech by Lloyd George, to Little Tich at the Manchester Hippodrome. In the 1920s, Einstein arrived in the city to deliver a lecture on Relativity, in German moreover. There was some perplexity in the *Manchester Guardian* office. Who could be sent to report this event? Nobody knew anything about Relativity; and Relativity expounded in German was a bit of a poser, to say the least. Crozier, acting editor on this crucial night in the reporters' room, remembered that Langford was a good German linguist. Langford agreed affably to go to Einstein's lecture and describe it to the length of three-quarters of a column. We waited in the 'Thatched House' for his return from the lecture, tense with expectation. He came into the bar at ten o'clock, and ordered his tankard of ale. Breathless we asked: 'How did you go on—could you grapple. . . . ?' 'Oh, yes', said Langford, taking his first swig. 'Yes, it wasn't too difficult. Einstein speaks good German.' 'We know he does', we impatiently retorted, 'he's a German himself. But what about this "Relativity"?' Langford pondered, then said: 'Interesting—aye, *interesting*. But all platitudes, all platitudes.' He produced a wonderful précis of the address, a thousand words, and caught the 11.45 tram to his home in Withington. 'All platitudes! . . .'

A flower show was on view in Manchester. Langford was naturally the man to deal with it for the paper. He merely mentioned the prize-winners, then proceded to digress as follows:

'The rose is the national flower of England, and supreme as it is among flowers, it feeds our pride in our country, and in ourselves, as no other flower. Flowers quicken the sense of beauty so greatly that the right love of them is almost one with the sense of romance; and for the romance that lies in the extravagance of beauty no flower will bear comparison with the rose. Few types of women, even, will sustain that comparison, although there are many types of roses. The rose bursts on us in the full pride of the summer, and is one with it, and is almost the essence of it. After it the summer has nothing further to reveal, for the gold of autumn is but decay, and even the carnation that might hold its own with any other flower, though it challenges the rose, and vies with it in every feature of scent and colour, equals it in none, and is by every single one of its charms sealed the rose's vassal. The rose, too, is among flowers the only fit emblem of life. Its blood is rich as our own, and any one who will put his cheek to the cheek of the rose under the summer sun will find that it takes a warmth literally comparable to that of life. To the lover the rose is the lip, the breath and the heart of his mistress in one, and the poets have given it this meed of praise times and in ways without number. Nor does the rose ever shame their extravagance. What other flower would sustain such comparison for an instant? And the rose runs the whole scale of beauty, from the blushing simplicity of the brier in which the dew finds a lucky cradle, to the crimson of the rose that vaunts herself the paramour of the midday sun.

'The rose can not only be a spendthrift of its charms, but is the one miser whose hoard can give intoxication. Who does not know the rose, deeper than all others, that cups its rich folds and compact scents until a box of spikenard would scarce vie with its rich odour? Again, by what marvellous power does the rich moss rose extract its sweets from its heart, and distil them on its rough coat, or the sweetbrier rose excel the sweetest of herbs? How did the tea-rose filch its odours of the East and retain them amid all the waters of the West, which use their powers in vain to wash them out? And the rose is not merely the most exquisitely scented and compact of flowers when it is not the most profuse and open-hearted, but it can be also the boldest and noblest of horned flowers, folding its petals to a spike of great nobility. In its climbing form it has a grace that would make it independent of flowers, and a plant for poets to sing of if it never had a bud. But in this form it becomes the most generous of all, and gives forth its blossoms by thousands until they overwhelm the dwelling over which they grow. The rose, not only in its beauty but in its thorns and its canker and in its death, is the theme of sentiment. When in its splendour it suddenly falls, it dies the most gorgeous death, and after death it does not cease to be cherished, nor do its sweets become extinguished.

> *Rose leaves, when the rose is dead,*
> *Are heap'd on the beloved's bed,*

sings Shelley. But we have vowed not to quote the poets, as their beautiful references to the rose run to many anthologies.'

A 'report' of a local flower show—and an example of Langford's discursiveness. Round about this same decade in the Golden Age of the *Manchester Guardian*, a vocalist made himself known to the paper by claiming he could sing baritone and tenor simultaneously. So the News Editor suggests this phenomenon should come to the office for an audition before Langford. The phenomenon and Langford retired into a room, closed doors. We reporters, and even one or two of the editorial intelligentsia, listened, curiosity-bound, outside. From the room we heard strange gurglings, high and low shocks on the glottis. After a short while Langford emerged from the room and informed the News Editor: 'This isn't a matter for a music-critic. It's a job for a plumber.'

Langford could not have manifested himself in any newspaper office of our present time. He wouldn't have 'involved' himself in anything. His news sense was unpredictable. Sir Thomas Beecham absented himself from the felicity of the conductor's rostrum for several years, getting his father's and his own affairs in order. His reappearance in a concert hall was, of course, a music-critic's 'must'. Sir Thomas 'reappeared' at a Hallé Concert. Critics attended this concert from various points of the national compass. Langford wrote a column—all about Brahms; he remembered, just in time, in his closing sentence, to state that Sir Thomas had conducted. Most likely—I can't exactly swear to it—he lost himself in Brahms' First Symphony, this way:

'Brahms, in his music, and especially in the C minor symphony, brings back music to the moral heights on which it had lived with Bach and Beethoven, but from which the later romantic movement had withdrawn it. The process of modernization in music has been almost wholly one of taking up the phases of secular life and of putting lyrical poetic feeling into music. Brahms did not lose this gift, but he restored also the heroic moral tone, which is part of classicism in music. But Brahms, like Goethe, and unlike the poets and composers with whom piety is a culture and a sentiment, never allows a moral sentiment to blind him to the truth, nor is he willing to plant his faith in the clouds, or in anything that he merely wishes to be true. He is simple in aesthetic; and his faith is childlike in that sense; but in every other sense he is a man. If we remember his *Song of Destiny* we shall remember especially a tremendous picture at its close where, in music that speaks louder than the words, his notes snap off and leave us with nothing but the sight of man falling from cliff to cliff into the abyss. The many terrible plucked notes which we hear from time to time in the C minor symphony have, one and all, no less portentous a meaning . . .'

Musik als Ausdruck, music as expression, music as an extension of man's consciousness. Such writing, done 'on the night', date stones thrown in, or rather, spat out, is nowadays outmoded. But we can read Langford yet with profit to mind and spirit, and with a reader's fascination. How much of the present-day 'analytical' music criticism is readable the day after it is printed, or intelligible except to a few who understand the lingo?

Langford did not conduct a post-mortem on the inert score of composition; he put the living, sounding musical organism under an X-ray. A great composition is not a patterned thing-in-itself, objectively presented and objectively to be contemplated. Music is *all* the composers who have created it; a symphony by Beethoven is as much, and more so, part of Beethoven as the voice of him heard when he was phenomenally alive. When we listen to music we taste the body of genius; take part in communion with genius. So much as this I learned from Langford. He once took a pianist to task for playing Beethoven's Op. 106 sonata *too* musically; he played it almost as music absolute, derived from song. If we accepted such a reading, argued Langford, we should have to protest against Beethoven's ineffectuality in this sonata. We should, from the pianist-in-question's interpretation, recoil in the first bar and regard Beethoven, throughout the first and second movement, as musically illiterate, for no pure musical ear would pound away on the keyboard in so unseemly a way. Langford then argued that it is the nature of song born of music to go up and down; repeated notes are ineffectual in it. But as the sonata absorbed his mind, so that he penetrated behind a 'surface' performance, he produced literature which soared above criticism of an occasion. 'For a profound, not formal melody, what is there in music so moving as the D major melody, whose first long phrase plumbs the depths of the piano, and whose anti-phonal strain is enskied and fraught with a divine consolation?' What an inspired and lovely word, in this context—'enskied'. Langford crowned this report of a routine concert in the following language (remember, writ in pencil, 'on the night', for a daily and necessarily perishable newspaper):

'The amazing thing is to feel that, after all, there is unity in such a sonata. The fact indicates that either the springs of joy and of sorrow are more closely related than we think, or that they are both so greatly softened by the ideality of art that we are able to pass from one to the other as in a dream which relates all things, not so much to life as to itself. One cannot pass over this movement' [the Adagio] 'without noting also the wonderful melismata, which at certain places transform the whole being of the melody. As tears transform life until a glistening joy breaks through the very sorrow of the heart, so do these evanescent particles of music, the harmonies and melodies of this divine music, transcend themselves. . . .'

Langford never wrote a book. He had no literary ambitions. When I collected an anthology of his myriad pieces from the *Manchester Guardian*, and the Oxford University Press published it forty years ago, it did not run to a second edition, and is today resting in the obscure limbo, the dark and backward abysm of forgotten books.

Another trait of Langford's psychological make-up enabled me to get on to his wavelength. He had an acute sense of the brevity of things that matter, things of passing, delightful and beautiful motion, in time or in space. As I have earlier recorded, I saw Karsavina in my early twenties, dancing in Stravinsky's *L'Oiseau de Feu*; the shimmering thrill of the whole of her being sent out currents of wondrous life, temperament, spirit and all the vital and enchanting elements of dance and consumingly vivacious presence. And as I saw it all, the illuminated stage and scene,

I felt a poignant ache of the heart; it is all passing from us, I thought, it is only a moment stolen. I did not know Goethe then. Langford, in some subterranean Manchester café, as we sat surrounded by Manchester cotton merchants playing dominoes, Langford first quoted to me Faust's 'Verweile doch, du bist so schön!' To catch, to hold the fleeting moment! Langford wrote, once and for all, of Beethoven's 'fallings away and vanishings' in the E Flat Piano Concerto: 'One might almost call it the sole aim of Beethoven's music to give it such intimations of immortality. If he gathers strength it is not for its own sake, but to have those wonderful diminuendo and pianissimo effects in his power with which he surprises us and makes us ask what kind of beings we must be to feel ourselves so much touched by the mere passing and vanishing of sound.'

His training in music at Leipzig tended to give him a preference for the German masters. *Die Meistersinger* was almost in his blood; he was himself kin with Hans Sachs. Music, he maintained, is an art of cadence and 'however bravely, as in the overture to *Die Meistersinger*, the banner of tone may be opened out, the cadence and the fall of music must come, and the most loving and humane tones at last must fall on the air. But that they may die as the ripeness of a reconciled humour, from which every essence of sourness has been strained, and of which nothing but the purest love of one's human kind remains, is a lesson more thoroughly to be learned by hearing an ideal performance of *Die Meistersinger* than by anything else that the arts have given us'.

Yet Langford was quick, half-a-century ago, to respond to the quiddity of Debussy's piano music. He pointed out that Debussy had enlarged the range and style of piano-playing because of his effects of shade and mass which have endowed the keyboard with a sublimity new to the instrument, a new sense of depth, altitude and distance. Not all the 'analysis' of the musicologist could describe and illuminate the Debussy Préludes so vividly and penetratingly and comprehensively as those three perfectly chosen words—depth, altitude and distance. He also got to the heart and fundamental creative chamber of Cesar Franck in a single paragraph, to the effect that Franck's music in general tells us not only the influence of the organ but also the influence of the cathedral architecture, with its Gothic and romantic, grotesque implications. In my ears remains to this day a remark of his about Franck, spoken probably in a café, tram or public bar: 'Franck discovered that a sort of bell sound might come in anywhere and harmonise the whole harmonic texture.' All said without the slightest show of egg-head talking down at a young listener; all said in the same tone and discursive, spontaneous way he had of talking of soccer, parliament or delphiniums. He could be sharp, even wounding in his conversation; he would test anybody introduced to him by a cutting thrust. 'If he can stand that, he'll be well worth knowing.' He was, as I've said, never witty in his writings, never obviously sarcastic. He chided me when, in emulating Newman, I wrote of some pianist with a brash ironic 'crack'. 'Never', he cautioned me, 'write anything about a performer that you wouldn't be prepared to say to him face to face.' Nothing pompous about him as he gave me this advice. In everyday talk his wit, like Falstaff's, was not only as much himself as his clothes (which I couldn't easily believe he ever got out of) but was the source of wit in others. At a dull performance of *Parsifal* he was moving about restlessly in his seat next to me. I whispered, in the dark auditorium, while the Grail Scene was in progress: 'Aren't you enjoying yourself?' 'No', he grunted, 'Amfortas is the wisest man in this theatre tonight—he has brought his bed with him.'

He was a persistent Goethean. He constantly reminded me of Goethe's verse-epigram about the old wiseacre who left a crowded party—we'd call it a cocktail party nowadays—went home, and when he was asked if he had enjoyed himself and met anybody, said: 'If they had been books, I shouldn't have read a page of them.' Langford seldom talked small, about the weather or your health. You might meet him in the street by chance, and at once he would say, or something in the same key: 'If I found English as difficult and involved as Henry James, I'd stick to my flowers altogether.'

I was at his bedside near his last hour. I sat with his wife, his destined companion and foil. At this time a writer in the *Manchester Guardian* was contributing a clever column under the initials 'W.G.'. Mrs. Langford asked, 'Who is "W.G."?' Before I could reply, the recumbent and, until now, sleeping and sinking Langford opened his eyes, murmuring, as though he had overheard our conversation from another world: 'W.G.? Why W.G. Grace, of course.' These were the last words I heard from him. His name is unknown in the Sunday market of book reviewers and music commuters. Nonetheless, he was a great and abundantly enriched man, enriched by nature, by living and by reading and by thinking, all taken in his stride, or rather, in his shuffle. I cherish every moment spent in his company, ironic shafts aimed at me and all.

EDWARDIAN MUSIC-HALL

In my youth, around 1905, the music-hall was abundant, a mirror held up to the life and habits of the nation, notably reflecting the joys, trials and domestic frustrations of the 'lower classes'. In every large city a Moss and Stolls Empire or Hippodrome was erected. The old Victorian variety saloon, with its affable, loquacious 'Chairman', became obsolete; into these new Empires and Hippodromes of plush and gilt, the family could respectably venture; comparatively venture, that is to say. There would be for them to view the presence and wink of Marie Lloyd, the 'Flossie' of the period in apotheosis, as though leaning over the gold bar of Heaven, beer-pumps of Paradise beside her. She would sing and tell us that 'our lodger's such a nice young man, a nice young man he is, so kind, so good to all our familee; he's never going to leave us, oh dear, oh dear, no. He's so sweet, so very very sweet,—mother tells me so.' All sung and acted with glances and gestures of unprintable imputations. George Robey, eyebrows admonishing; Eugene Stratton, 'coon' singer, with his husky voice, dancing on air and haunting our ears with 'Little Dolly Daydream' and 'Lily of Laguna', melodies still in the air. Only yesteryear I heard 'Lily of Laguna', sung in the near distance, wafted over the moonlit water, as the liner I was voyaging in was anchored outside Colombo, and I leant over the ship's side.

There was Cinquevalli juggling with heavy (or they looked heavy) cannon balls; there was the funny man, supposed to be a waiter in a restaurant, who came on the stage carrying a terrific pile of plates. He held the plates in his hands, trying to keep them in position with pressure from his chin. He swayed this way, that way. The plates wriggled, describing a mark of interrogation. Then they crashed, split asunder, to the exalted liberation of our born, innate and tyrannical regard for order and the eternal fitness of things; also, at the same time, liberating the imp of destruction residing in everybody worthwhile. The funny waiter, after contemplating the wreckage of pottery minutely, extricated a hammer from his coat-tails and proceeded to smash each plate that had somehow escaped intact from the general destruction.

Every week we would, towards Friday, look at the hoardings in Manchester to find out what allurements had been conjured for us next Monday and following nights. The music-hall announcements on the hoardings contained three decisive classifications; top of the bill, middle of the bill and bottom of the bill. Top and bottom were representative, or indicative, of performers supposedly possessing equal powers of box-office attraction. I have known music-hall posters heralding Robey at the top of the bill, with Wilkie Bard or Gertie Gitana at the bottom. Yet between 'top' and 'bottom' there was some subtle, almost feudalistic difference; Robey, Vesta Tilley, Little Tich never were names at the bottom. The nomination for the 'middle' of the bill usually referred to some talent potential enough to remain for a time being weighed in the balance, in a sort of purgatory of public esteem.

Little Tich! His name was really Relph and, I believe, he had some French blood in him. He was small in physical stature, but he did not exploit dwarfish traits. He wore long, flapping boots, over which he would lean as he took the audience into his confidence. He presumed baldness, sported a bow tie and a top, shiny hat, upon which he would breathe, then polish with a sleeve. And, as he breathed, he would advertise his bronchitis. Like most of his famous contemporary comedians, Robey, Weldon, George Formby and Harry Tate, Tich was an actor; he did not set out obviously 'to be funny'. He did not, in the manner of most latter day T.V. comedians, laugh at his own humour. In fact, the T.V. comedians are usually the first to laugh. And Tich, and the rest of the music-hall makers of fun, did not use a microphone. Imagine Robey reprimanding an audience via microphone: 'Desist! I am not here as a source of public flippancy. I'm surprised at *you*, Ag-er-nes!' Only to think of Stratton gliding over the boards as though bodilessly thrown by the limelight; only to think of him, microphoned, singing 'Little Dolly Daydream, pride of Idaho'—to think thus is blasphemy of cherished memories. Tich, like his colleagues, was essentially serious; the laughter he provoked came as a by-product of an accurately observed impersonation of life.

I remember his presentation of a prosecuting counsel, be-wigged and gowned, ironically obsequious before the court, unctuous in speech with 'M'luds', and grappling with briefs and precedents. He had charm, a common characteristic of the comedians of his period. Whenever he took a curtain he would bow quickly and capaciously over his extended boots, and his bow would be so suddenly and so gratefully acknowledging that he would knock himself out as his bald head collided with the stage. Once I laughed at him so convulsively that I fell off my seat at a pantomime at the Manchester Palace theatre (I confess I was then only ten years old). Tich was one of the Ugly Sisters in *Cinderella*, and they had not received tickets of invitation for the ball. A flunkey attendant refused them admission. In a swift burst of inspiration, Tich said: 'I know!—let's walk in backwards, and they'll think we're coming out.'

Wilkie Bard, as a charwoman, came down the stage, carrying a bucket of soapsuds and a cleaning cloth. He went down on his (or her) knees, and made a wide wet circle on the floor with the cloth, indicating the immediate sphere of the cleansing operations. Then, suddenly, he would rise from her knees, come before the footlights, and announce by song, in a soft contralto voice, that 'I want to sing in Opera', thus confiding in us a lofty but natural ambition.

Harry Tate, as a 'city' man, came bustling into his office, moustaches working rapidly, and saying to the staff: 'Good morning, good morning, good morning!' 'No letters this morning?' he said. 'Very well, then; we must write some.' All done very seriously and not apparently conscious of an audience.

There is only one comedian alive today, as I write on Sunday, January 25, 1970, who could go into the company of the masters of the high-noon of the music-hall. He is Frankie Howerd. Maybe I should add the names of Harry Worth and Al Read.

George Formby (senior) certainly mingled with the greatest depicters of Lancashire character and climate of the 'depression' years. He was Lowry in advance of Lowry, pale of face, scarecrow thin, muffler and shapeless clothes covering his undernourished frame. Probably his major meal at night before bedtime, as a boy, had been 'pobs'; to produce 'pobs' a thick round of white loaf was cut into cubes and put into a basin. Tea was then poured into it, with sugar and condensed milk added, the whole of these constituents churned by a spoon into a congested mess, nicely calculated to keep hunger at bay till morning—as I can well testify. George Formby would come on to the stage tentatively, look around and find the conductor of the music-hall orchestra, find him rather to his surprise. 'Good evn'in', Alf', he would say, adding, 'Ah'm a bit tight on chest tonight, but Ah think Ah can mannidge.' The voice quavered as it put up the fight. Laughter contested pathos. He would sing that he was standing at the corner of the street, starry-eyed, hoping for romance in the guise of a blond. When he danced it was as though he was recurrently seized by dizziness and weakness of legs. As I say, Lowry pre-Lowry. Lowry himself emerged from the Lancashire scene which Formby made visible. Lowry knocked at doors, as I did, trying to sell insurance burial policies to slum denizens who could hardly afford to keep alive.

Welfare State! Grants for students of art, literature and culture in general? R. H. Spring sold evening newspapers in a Welsh town when he was at school in the daytime, supporting a widowed mother. Who writes and paints for us now, knowing anything fundamental about life at the bone? University dons who have never sung 'Lily of Laguna', or avidly eaten (or drunk) 'pobs', or stood at the corner of the street, tight on chest, but dreaming dreams of escape?

Every night, up and down the land, these old-time comedians had to hold the attention of vast audiences by means of individual talent and presence, and by their own unmicrophoned voices. And the audiences in the Empires, Tivolis, Palaces and Hippodromes could be brutal in response. Pennies were thrown from the galleries to the stage occupied by some lonely, pitiful, incompetent performer. I have myself thrown an egg at an un-funny comedian in the Tivoli theatre, once situate in Peter Street, Manchester. A small company of us boys, housed in bath-less, unlavatoried houses in Rusholme and Moss Side, would go to the Tivoli gallery. We saved weekly from our earnings as carriers and fetchers, handcart pullers, sub-clerks, newspaper sellers in the streets; and before invading the Tivoli, we 'clubbed' our financial assets and bought a supply of eggs, sharing them equitably. In those days there were, as Dan Leno (greatest of comedians next to Charlie Chaplin) pointed out, three categories of eggs: new laid, fresh—and eggs. It was an 'egg' that I threw at the unfunny man on the stage of the Manchester Tivoli Theatre in 1905; and I hit him in his middle-stump with a brilliant throw from long-on in the gallery.

The three greatest comedians, Chaplin, Leno and George Formby (senior), shared the secret way of mingling pathos with comic appeal; each showed to us the 'little' man, the product of an un-affluent State, rich as Croesus or poor as church mice, according to the position in life to which one had been called, so we were clerically informed, by God. The 'little man' looking for some sign of romantic colour in his encircling drabness of environment, waiting and waiting, catching a glimpse; then, like Chaplin in his first 'silent' and most cherishable showings, departing to the distance, alone, shoulders hunched and de-pressed until, suddenly, he flicked his cane, thrust one foot outward, as another romantic hope stirred him.

If the comedian, or music-hall performer of any kind, did not have true powers of the actor, he was soon herded among the 'middle of the bill' mediocrities. As I say, Chaplin, Leno and Formby could be humanly touching. At the extreme of these was Grock, an entirely unexpected and fantastic visitation to music-halls of Britain; foreign, of course. Grock was the most complete and consummatory of all clowns, tall with an egg-shaped forehead, and with a long chin which he would project to express determination or coyness, according to changing circumstances. The first impression he conveyed to us was of shyness, as he sidled on to the stage from the rear, wearing trousers tight and long, a large collar with a striped bow, coat-tails and flat oversized boots. As he came before us, he staggered under the weight of a fiddle-case big enough to contain a double-bass. After he had removed from his back this apparently insupportable burden he opened the case and produced from it the tiniest violin imaginable. This was not a trick obviously contrived to get laughter of the unexpected from the audience alone. Grock himself was clearly as much surprised and delighted as ourselves at his discovery of so enchantingly tiny a violin. He made soft gurgles of delight; his red mouth described the outlines of a quivering letter V. He never spoke an organised dictionary language; but he could be expressive and eloquent with onomatopoeia. Only once did he utter, during his performance, a recognisable verbal sound. He performed with what the programme named as his 'Partner', a sleek, tailored young man who played a violin (a standard violin, if not a Strad). Grock, at the piano, was concerned with something or other wrong about the concert grand, opening the lid and looking within. The 'Partner', impatient to begin a piece, struck the top of the piano with his bow, whereat Grock, looking up sharply and over his shoulder, cried out: 'Come in!'

Grock's 'Partner' was a perfect foil to Grock, shiny and well-oiled of hair, serious and manifestly ambitious as a solo violinist; but finding Grock not an easy, adjustable collaborator. A problem arose as soon as 'Partner' joined Grock on the stage, a problem arising from the positions of the piano and the piano stool, standing yards apart. Grock, with all the good-will in the world, put his strength and shoulders to the bulk of the 'Steinway' grand pianoforte and strove, might and main, to push it towards the stool. When the sleek young 'Partner' very condescendingly lifted up the stool, carried it and placed it in front of the keyboard, the most embracing smile of illumination spread over Grock's face. He was enchanted. Grock, indeed, was constantly finding out things for the first time. From the moment he came into the scene, Grock unmistakably was a being out of another dimension, yet nonetheless a visitant

humanly related, and willing to learn. He sat down at last at
the piano, the 'Partner' chafing to impress us on his violin.
Grock ran his fingers over the keyboard. The 'execution', the
fingering, seemed not to please him, the tone was lacking in
brilliance. Then he discovered that he was wearing thick wool-
len gloves. So he took them off and played the scales again. His
smile now became beatific. He drew his 'Partner's' attention—
and, indirectly ours—to the phenomenon; with his bare fingers
he could play much better. We could infer that he had, until
this very revelatory moment, played the piano all his life in
gloves.

'Partner' here left the stage to Grock, who produced from
somewhere a concertina. He climbed onto a chair, an ordinary
cane chair, and sat on the curved back of it, knees crossed, a
most precariously balanced position. He leaned towards the
footlights, and, after a deep intake of breath, blew them out,
left to right. A single 'lime' shone on his face in the prevailing
darkness. He prepared himself to play the concertina. His fingers pressed the keys; and, faintly, we could hear the beginning
of the quartet from *Rigoletto*. What is more, Grock was hearing
it too. He listened intently. He looked around and up and down,
seeking the source of the music. When he had traced it to the
concertina, which he held far from his body in the truly professional manner, his chuckle of enchanted surprise was more
and more gurglingly onomatopoeic.

Next, he indicated to the conductor that he was, at long last,
really ready for serious playing, with full orchestral accompaniment. The conductor raised his arms and baton. And before the
orchestra could begin a note, there was a crash, a splitting noise,
not merely of wood and of cane, but as of a whole universe, the
bottom dropping out of it. Grock had crashed clean through
the chair at this moment of the conductor's, the orchestra's, and
everybody else's suspense.

Clowns have from time to time immemorial sat on chairs and
fallen off, have sat on hats. Grock sat on his own violin, exactly
as he fell through the chair. The traditional clown played prac-
tical jokes on other folk, scoring over them because of superior
knowledge. The clown's traditional 'booby traps' were played

by Grock on Grock himself; they didn't score over *him*. He was happy to run into them. He found his tiny fiddle in the enormous case like a child finding its little toe for the first time, bubbling with pleasure. Grock made the fantastic—and the humanly likeable—companionable. In our strange complicated world he was willing to learn, but often rather at a loss. In private life, Grock was Swiss. He broke off relations with and engagements in this country because he objected to our ideas about income tax. He was, at any rate, not going to be taken in by that.

MUSIC-MAKERS

Paderewski

The young critics of gramophone records, recording angels of the Higher Fidelity, seem often to patronise Paderewski's piano playing, as they lend ears to discs made decades ago. Even the latest recording technology can reproduce only the material, and not the personal, not to say spiritual, content or presence of an actual interpretation of music. Paderewski, of course, played in a style considered nowadays rather old-fashioned, romantic, left hand sometimes not apparently knowing what the right hand was doing; but it is a comic aspect of the present 'sophisticated' and 'permissive' age that it has been endowed with a wisdom and insight into human mind and psychology not lavished on any preceding, or immediately preceding, generation. In the heyday of Paderewski, civilisation could turn to such teachers and stimulators of thought as, to name a few, Tolstoy, Herbert Spencer, Huxley and Shaw. Karl Marx was still an urgent influence; there were also Freud, Bertrand Russell, not to mention 'popular' educators such as H. G. Wells. Where in all the world of the 1970s is there one obviously great influential thinker, inspiring the young idea. Muggeridge in England? David Frost? In music criticism Paderewski in this country had to survive as pianist the critical investigations of Newman, Langford and Runciman.

I heard Paderewski for the last time in 1928, when he played at a Saturday night concert in Manchester. He was sixty-two years old, but was corporeally surrounded by the time-weary halo of his legend. No musician has had a reputation as world-

37

and class-encompassing as Paderewski, a reputation spread everywhere without the modern advertisements of television, radio and the rest. People in two hemispheres, knowing nothing of music at all, were aware of Paderewski—cab-drivers and Royalty alike. As I saw Paderewski walking on to the platform this October Saturday night of 1928, I and the audience could feels rays of his mind, nature, experience and being coming to us like light-waves. The hall was semi-darkened, and a glow of artificial illumination touched his noble mane of hair, now greying. His face was lined and melancholy. Already he was a visitant from a receding epoch.

If I remember well, this recital began with the 'Études Symphoniques' of Schumann. Of course I remember well, because of the surprise stirred in me by his almost unromantic treatment of Schumann. His tone was hard and keen. I had been told, years before this recital, that Paderewski frequently saw to it, before giving a concert, that the hammers of his piano were severely flayed so that there should be no obscurities of tones or overtones when he touched the keyboard. As a consequence, he gave us an etched Schumann; in fact, while playing Schumann Paderewski might well have been a thorough-going purist, insisting on a percussiveness suitable for Stravinsky. But, along with a quite unsentimental tone for Schumann, he would indulge in pauses, dwelling on phrases with a lingering of fingers which entirely contradicted the impersonal sounds emanating from the instrument.

His Chopin playing remains cherishable in my memory for a rare and special cause. He could play Chopin without a weakening of the essential fibre of the music. Where there is keenness of melodic flight, there can be no sentimental dalliance. Never did Paderewski let us hear Chopin in flight with a broken wing. So fine was his musical poise that he could afford to linger over the main theme of the G minor Ballade. Indulgence was not weakness here; this order of dalliance with rhythm could be taken as a sign of Paderewski's aristocratic pride of musicianship, slave to no letter of the score, kin with the aristocratic breeding of Chopin himself.

The lasting impression, to me, of Paderewski's farewell was

an interpretation of the A Flat Sonata of Beethoven's Op. 110. He withdrew entirely from the audience during this work, in which Beethoven himself seems to be taking a farewell from the outer world. The thematic material in part glances back on Beethoven's past. The Adagio has that sense of silence which in Beethoven's late period was his own secret, the meaning of which the wisest of us can hear as music only. We can but ask ourselves: 'God knows what Beethoven is saying now; to whom in the name of all things mysterious is he talking?' Paderewski's tone in this passage—can I hear it yet?—seemed to lose contact with the world of our senses. Tone somehow went out of his playing. It became shadelike; it was audible meditation. The playing was abstract, metaphysical, so much tone spun out of the stuff of a troubled mind. The sonata lifted the concert above the familiar routine; the performance let us understand that Paderewski, if his original romanticism had not by age been changed altogether to the ripeness of the philosophic mind, could, when he was moved to it, put vain things away from him and go into the company of the gods, and stand amongst them, and talk with them in their own language.

Arrau

One afternoon, during an Edinburgh Festival, I came upon Claudio Arrau sitting in the lounge of the Caledonian Hotel, taking tea without obvious enthusiasm. He had just arrived from New York, after a difficult and exhausting flight. He proposed going to bed early, an unusual procedure for him. I asked if we could lunch together next day. Oh dear, no; he would need to practise. He was giving a recital the day after, a Saturday. 'But surely', I insisted, 'you could spare an hour or two?' 'No', he said, his eyes widening to large circles, 'I have to play the Études of Chopin.' 'Good Lord, Claudio', I retorted, 'you must have played the Études hundreds of times!' 'Maybe', he answered, 'maybe, but they are very difficult.'

This expression of humility from a master pianist touched me greatly. Arrau is like that; I have known no renowned musician as modest as Arrau. At the height of his career he abruptly cancelled an engagement involving a performance of the D minor Concerto of Mozart. He had played the work many times in different concert halls the world over. He now, after his fiftieth year, decided that he required deeper study into the music to get him closer to the heart of the matter. He is a compound of seriousness and light-heartedness, of wisdom and quite boyish hilarity, of ripe age and constant and spontaneous youth. At the piano, he sends out the impression of an artist persistently searching for the hidden essence. His fingers seem to dig into the bed of the keyboard, as though his mind, by means of his technique, were endeavouring to root out the ultimate secret.

40

Arrau the musical thinker often subdues Arrau the playboy and hedonist. He, born in Chile, can make music (of all sorts) sound as German as anything sung by Fischer-Dieskau. This same ageless Arrau has, in company with him at dinner, removed years from my shoulders, from my heart and mind, by sheer spirit of fun and delight. We were given a menu, in a Scottish restaurant, printed in French. Immediately I parodied Souzay and a recital of songs by Fauré, Duparc and so on, singing 'Blanchaille Diable', 'Ratatouille Niçoise', 'Les Fromages Assortis', 'La Coquille de Fruits de Mer', and, quick as the quickest-moving wavelength, Arrau jumped to the cue, and achieved an enchantment of impersonation and satire. He *was* Souzay; and the menu was a copy of all French songs that came to his vivacious and encyclopaedic memory. His tastes in music, literature and the theatre are wide, ranging from the best 'musical' to the latest of Brecht. I have yet to strike a blind spot in his cultural equipment. He could, I fancy, place, from memory, the position in any gallery in the world any masterpiece, canvas or sculpture, tell you where it is hanging or where standing. This same profoundest of living interpreters of Beethoven could be seen—*was* seen by myself—in a Woolworth store, inspecting every gadget, tin-openers or whatever, as though every one were a precious object or relic, glass-cased in a very select museum.

I first heard him play, round about the 1920s, at a 'popular' Saturday night concert in a series given every winter by a Manchester man called Brand Lane, an orchidaceous *entrepreneur*, who occasionally conducted a local choir of his own formation in *Messiah* at Christmas, beating out the tempo firmly and conscientiously. His Saturday evenings were looked down upon by subscribers to the Hallé Concerts; nonetheless, he engaged singers, fiddlers and pianists whose fees soared well beyond the financial resources of the Hallé—Chaliapine, Kubelik, Tauber, Galli-Curci. His most incredible achievement was to lure Jeritza (in her prime) from Vienna to Manchester on a foggy November night. She sang with piano accompaniment; and Brand Lane had footlights on the platform, and coloured overhead 'limes'. He would lead his women artists to the platform through a garden of pot-plants in full bloom, handing them over to audiences, for which introductory purpose he wore white gloves. These 'star' personages did not, of course, begin the evening's proceedings; their advent, or manifestation, was prepared by some dim satellite, usually a pianist. Gerald Moore once marked time before an audience impatient to hear, and see, Chaliapine. Moore was the overwhelmed anonymous accompanist; but as a curtain-raiser to the main event, he actually tackled Bach-Busoni.

At such a concert Arrau, in his early twenties, became acquainted with concert goings-on in England. I forget who was the 'big business' attraction this time, obviously somebody glamorous, or I should not have been present, because I paid for my ticket. I was at the time reporter on the *Manchester Guardian*, with my music-critic's career and ambition rather a long way ahead. I recall the occasion mainly to mention that, after Arrau had performed his menial part, I saw Langford applauding, the venerable critic of the 'M.G.' clapping his hands, a sight seldom witnessed and never foreseen. Langford was the first critic in this country to write of Arrau as a young artist of the keyboard blessed with rare gifts. Langford also 'discovered' Schnabel while temporarily withdrawing his attention from the Mahler Festival in Amsterdam in 1920.

Nearly twenty years passed by, following my first raw hearing of Arrau, before I wrote of his playing in my office of music-critic of the *Manchester Guardian*, at a concert in Manchester given just as Hitler and his cohorts were getting busy. Manchester's main concert hall was taken over by the army; the 'phoney' war had begun with the blackouts, tense and intimidatory. Arrau now played in a cinema; he would then be arriving at the mid-forties of his life, I wrote of him somewhat as follows:

'On the whole he gave us an enchanting Schumann; and how enchanting "Carnaval" can be, if it is played with each piece created for us anew, as though the pianist were reflecting, and as though fancy were his guide and inspiration. There is an art, which few pianists command, of seeming to enter a miniature piece and mould it from within, shaping the melodies, rhythms and harmonies from some private chamber of imagination. It is easy to convey the impression that you are presenting "Carnaval" from the outside, as merely a miscellaneous collection of "pictures" or "portraits". If Arrau, not being German of the departed old world, was unable entirely to recapture the right mood of warm, *gemütlich* romance, he already can come close to it, and would get closer if he could soften his outlines. He tends to emphasise, to bend too low over the keyboard, too studiously.'

I drag this passage from the limbo of Langford's emulative successor to enjoy, at this time of my life, the satisfaction of having prophetically, thirty years ago, touched on the basic-qualities of Arrau's art, and on the defects of those qualities. He is, for all his variegated characteristics as a man, a pianist seriously dedicated, more and more as the years try hard to push him prominently into the seventies. I think he would play our National Anthem rather as a hymn of some austerity. The style is not *always* the man himself. There are great pianists whose art is born of the keyboard, lives and revels and belongs to the keyboard, is, in fact, continued by and dedicated to the keyboard—Artur Rubinstein, for example. Arrau transcends the piano; he seems often to symphonise it, if I may use a word which is not my best English. He is not fulfilled, as an imaginative and thinking searcher in music, by the keyboard's range of tone, or by its accumulated 'association values', its tonal and rhythmical vocabulary, so to speak. He is at his freest and most imaginatively liberated while playing a piano concerto; here the canvas, the space-time territory, give him scope for complete involvement of his first-class musical brain, his quick response to introvert and extrovert promptings from composers as large-minded and as strong in sinew as Beethoven and the Brahms of the D minor and B Flat masterpieces. I am not under-rating Arrau as soloist, as a recital pianist. I have heard him explore and make musically audible and visual the keyboard world of the Liszt sonata—realise it in a comprehensive interpretation which presented Liszt in the round, his grandeur and his grandiosity.

I bring back to memory, as I write of Arrau now, a recital at an Edinburgh Festival of the Chopin Préludes. No doubt he approached the Préludes with the humility which caused him to genuflect in the presence, before performance, of the Études. As a fact, he took a firm grip on Chopin and urged him along his own forgetive way. ('Forgetive' in the Shakespearean meaning of the word, indicative of a driving, unyielding, personal, creative energy.) Most of us, critics and concert-public, have been listening to Chopin recitals a lifetime, revelling in delights to the ear that hurt not. Arrau challenged tradition and custom, shaking the dust from the Préludes, shaking easily recognisable identity from them. He portrayed a masculine Chopin, big-fisted, broad-chested, and strong of muscle, capable of putting George Sand in her place. After one of Pachmann's Chopin recitals, he was seen, in the artist's room, dotingly kissing his fingers. Arrau could, with equal pride, have kissed or caressed his biceps, wrists; caressed, or got somebody else to kiss, his forehead, behind which resides as finely yet powerfully textured a musical intelligence as any dowered on a pianist since Busoni and Schnabel.

To begin with, Arrau enlarged the formal stature of the Préludes. Wagner once foolishly described Chopin as a piano composer for the right hand. The centre of gravity in Arrau's playing of the Préludes was, and still is, the harmonic fundamentals, the part-writing, the polyphony, which is evidence of Chopin's seminal acquaintance with Bach. Arrau reveals, actually over-emphasises, a Chopin of wider tonal range than was ever dreamed of in the heyday of the nineteenth-century romantic indulgence and permissiveness. As I have given my ears to Arrau in Chopin, I confess I have, catching breath, whispered, 'O, for a whiff of Cortot's perfume'. Arrau, as he investigated the Préludes, on the Edinburgh occasion etched in my memory, gave the impression temporarily of sharing my own difficulty mentally to readjust notions of the Chopin style.

The first Prélude came from his fingers and forearms truly ponderous; then an unforgettable treatment of the second—in A minor—told us what manner of Chopin we were soon to hear and to meet. The crab-like left hand figure, and the dark hard chordings, were as though they were being scooped out of some tough, resisting tonal material by a keyboard sculptor's sharp scalpel. The Vivace, which came next for Arrau's approbation, acquired a wonderful fluency and clearness; but the tone remained unplastic and unsmiling. And the 'Majorca' Largo, in E minor, though noble in shape and diction in every deliberately moulded phrase, lacked the shades and softening contours which cause this music to wring the heart with its suggestions of remote or receding beauty in an autumnal loneliness, poignant with the 'pathos of distance'.

I have always made a distinction between a performance of music and an *experience* of music which transcends the notes of the score, and transcends also even the most expert technical skill. An 'experience' of music extends one's awareness to what a composer is saying; an 'experience' of music goes into the responsive listener's mind and stays there. This Chopin recital by Arrau I can 'experience' by memory to this day; I have already forgotten the significance of a piano recital given the other week by—what's his name?—well, never mind.

All the time, as Arrau moved from Prélude to Prélude, the miracle was happening; the greater Chopin emerged. To myself I said, great Heaven, to think that this music once reposed in the satchels of young ladies going to or from college and conservatoire of music; to think that this Chopin, severely a musical thinker in his twenties, and in the Études already prophetic of future tonal and harmonic direction, was once upon a time supposedly presented 'in the round', in all his aspects, by the amiable magician Pachmann! In Arrau's conceptual and technical control, the second Prélude foreshadowed none other than Bartók. I write now with impressions and perfumes of long ago renewed:

'Und mich ergreift ein längst entwöhntes Sehnen
Nach jenem stillen, ernsten Geisterreich . . .'*

*And I am seized by a long-lost yearning for that grave and silent spirit-world . . .

Cortot played Chopin as though all the world's lovers and their mistresses were in his audience. Paderewski played Chopin as though before Royalty. One mellow late summer evening I went to the Bösendorfersaal in Vienna to pick up tickets for a Rosenthal piano recital. From the distance, from a room upstairs, I heard the closing phrases of the Chopin E major Nocturne (the second of Op. 62); the notes fell as softly, immaterially and as autumnally as the September leaves from the trees in the Ringstrasse outside. The cadences went into my heart; they told of a gracious day going to an end. Arrau plays Chopin as though Chopin were contemporaneous with him; in fact, as though the shade of Bartók himself might be hovering approvingly near.

There are pianists—Artur Rubinstein and Horowitz—whose fingers seem dyed by the stain of the keyboard palette they work in; they woo our impressionable senses. In the fingers of Arrau you could swear that his brain is projected, an active, presently active, brain. There is little of nostalgia in his playing —this, perhaps, is the reason why I sometimes cannot keep on his wave-length. At my time of life nostalgia, and indulgence in the sense that time giveth and time taketh away, is a ripe harvest of civilised living. Played by Arrau, the brief flower-poised fragrance of the seventh Prélude sheds no leaf and has no fragrance; but with the 'Molto agitato' of the F sharp minor Prélude, Arrau's transforming genius urges Chopin decades ahead of his epoch. The figuration of hurrying, plunging notes is charged with power and clarity. I doubt if I would have even tried to share Arrau's conception of Chopin when I was, say, twenty-five years old, and ready to have my sensibilities wooed. Today I can realise that Arrau, alone of pianists, presents to us Chopin the full man, artist and strong-fibred musician. Indeed, I must confess that I see no future for Chopin, unless generations of today and tomorrow are led to understand that Chopin was made of sterner stuff than was ever conjectured in the Paris salons in which Chopin certainly was not born or in any way nurtured. There can be no richer tribute to Arrau than to say that his playing embodies Chopin in almost full musical range, in all of Chopin's astounding keyboard spectrum. Only the

46

perfume is missing here and there. He can revivify the hackneyed A flat Ballade, dower grandeur on the music. His treatment of the F minor Fantasie is truly majestic in its sweep and felicitous tone and finger touch, crowned by bold, not to say defiant, marching rhythms.

Hear, too, Arrau playing the Études. Now there is no dichotomy, no conflict between his initial approach and established style and diction. Arrau, in the Études, renders the music ageless and kin with all the music and all that can never become dated or 'period'. He knows the secret whereby interpretation by an artist goes beyond personal reactions, aesthetic or other. He is blessed by the gift of selfless involvement, the gift whereby rare and individual musical understanding and masterful technique can serve as a sort of entranced medium through which the poet-composer speaks—sometimes in reverberating prose and blank verse.

Rubinstein

As I write these words Artur Rubinstein is, by the reckoning of the calendar, an octogenarian. The spring of youth is in all his movements; his white hair stands erect on his forehead as though electrically charged. He runs up the steps to the concert platform easily and lightly, and walks to the awaiting piano quickly, yet without hurry. A friend asked him the other day: 'Artur, have you discovered the secret of eternal youth?' 'No', replied Rubinstein, 'No, and if I had discovered it, I would sell it.'

He is the complete pianist; his art begins in and from the keyboard, never strains or abuses it, even if his fortissimi can evoke a Jovian connotation. He does not venture beyond the scope of his instrument into some loftier dimensions of music, as, say, Schnabel did and Arrau does. Sometimes it is hard to say if Rubinstein is giving us an interpretation thought out in itself or if it is entirely a by-product of his playing, judged strictly as an artist-pianist's involvement in the keyboard. Not that he ever displays his comprehensive technique for its own astonishing sake. But we feel that Rubinstein approaches his composers, gets to the music's source, through the piano exclusively. He was nurtured at a time when any artist was expected to observe fidelity to his medium and not to go against its natural limitations, wherein, as a fact, its strength and potentialities could be found. He is an Old Master unenslaved by tradition, belonging *au fond* to the Seigneurial school of the nineteenth-century virtuosi; none the less, there is a vital difference marking him off

from what Nietzsche called the fluent-fingered pianist cavaliers
—'die Schule der Geläufigkeit'—adding with a Mephisto after-
thought, 'nach Frauen'. Rubinstein has sensibility and elasticity
of style. His experience in the school of Stravinsky brought lasting
astringency to his playing; so, as a consequence, his rhythm
seldom weakens into middle-aged, dandruffed languor and
sentiment. It is hardly pertinent to praise Rubinstein's playing
of Chopin; and it would be impertinent not to mention it in any
attempt to appraise his art. He reproduces the proper Chopin
texture, the aristocratic romantic content, a melody which has
a firm wing. A legato passage by Rubinstein has a lovely flight;
you can almost appreciate the dot on the crotchet which wings
the way of a phrase. His fingers go to the keyboard as though
by instinct. At times he turns his head and eyes upward, as if he
were listening—not to the sounds which *we* can hear, but to
overtones he himself is aware of in some inner chamber of his
consciousness.

When he plays an Intermezzo of Brahms, he reminds us that
of all instruments the piano is the most apt for the expression of
intimate thoughts—a reminder we most of us stand often in
need of at the moment. The late piano pieces of Brahms, like
the last four songs of Strauss, are the composer's matured
essence. Nobody today plays the Brahms Op. 117 with as much
as Rubinstein's inwardness. His tone, with twilight gradations,
puts each piece into a session of silent thought; which is a compliment indeed to offer to any pianist, especially to a maestro
who, like Rubinstein, can excite us with a 'Mephisto' Waltz of
Liszt, and causes us to remember, as he plays the 'Fantasiestücke'
of Schumann, that Joachim said of the composer that he was
'a young man writing with a golden pen'. I would not wish him
to go too habitually into mature Beethoven. I have heard him
transform the 'Appassionata' Sonata so that we could see, with
the ear, the music's nerve and muscle in play, as in the poise,
prance and spring of a racehorse; all that was missing was the
daemon. Rubinstein avoids the heavily accented diction of the
old school (with or without 'die Frauen'). For all his virtuoso
feathers he observes restraint of expression; the diminished
seventh announcement in the attack on the 'Appassionata'

49

Sonata was not, from Rubinstein's fingers, at all suggestive of the apocalyptic. It was beautifully shaded in tone, simply that and nothing more. Rubinstein is a master whose art needs no forcing; here ripeness is all. I have heard him play the G flat Impromptu of Schubert with a touch so light, yet capable of transition where the young god catches on high the sad echoes from the troublous regions below, a tone which if, after dying, anyone of us wakes to hear, we shall at once know that we have arrived in the right place.

Schnabel

Schnabel as pianist was at Rubinstein's extreme, expressing through the piano his intellectual and emotional way of life—which he could have done equally well on an organ. To say this I do not fall into the current mistake of ranking Schnabel as technically an insecure pianist at all. He could encompass the keyboard with a show of *Fingerfertigkeit*; but his fingers were on the small side, so that wide skips sometimes had to be negotiated by diplomatic rather than by technical extremes. He shared as a man Rubinstein's brand of Jewish wit. A gifted young pianist came to Schnabel hoping to be taught by him. Schnabel gave the young man an audition and was pleased. 'Yes, you have talent. Very promising. I should like to give you lessons.' The student hesitated, and diffidently asked what was Schnabel's fee a lesson. 'Five guineas.' The student dropped mouth and shoulders. 'I couldn't afford it', he said. 'Ah', replied Schnabel cheerfully, 'that is alright. I also give lessons at three guineas.' Then he added: 'But I don't recommend them.'

After a recital in Manchester I saw him in the Midland Hotel. 'Tonight', he declared, 'I played like a pig.' I protested: 'But Schnabel, you were splendid. And the audience—they were raving with applause.' 'Audiences', pronounced Schnabel, 'applaud, even when it is good.' He was so self-masterful, so charged with a well-stocked mind warmed by wit, that I was astounded to learn that he died unhappily, not only because of a heavy burden of physical disease, but with a mind clouded pessimistically. Some hints of this gloom of intellectual awareness I received during a train journey in his company from Manchester to London, round about the 1930s. We sat in the restaurant car; in those halcyon days you could enjoy a restaurant car on the railways of Great Britain in more or less solitary relaxation and comfort. For four hours Schnabel spoke of the menace of Hitler, at the time a menace no bigger a warning sign in the sky of our civilisation than a man's hand. Schnabel foresaw all the wrath to come; also he foresaw the mechanisation of the arts, the Admass proliferation of the arts, the de-individualising of the individual, the advent of the computer, mechanical and human. He also suffered disillusionment as a composer. He was more dedicated, if this were a possible trait in his psychological make-up, to composition than to piano playing. The inexplicable feature of his compositions is that he, classic in his general reactions to music, out-atonalised Schönberg so drastically that compared with Schnabel's music, Schönberg's is atonalism leavened with his mother's milk.

Schnabel was one of the acutest thinkers I have known among musicians, never talking trivialities. There was in him a fascinating mingling of modesty and conceit. He liked you to think he seldom practised at the keyboard; but on one occasion he told me: 'Next week I practise six hours every day.' 'Heavens', I said, 'really?' (to humour him). 'Yes, my next concert I have to play Mozart.' He did not play much Chopin; his touch was not for Chopin. But in Vienna a critic took him to task for neglecting Chopin, pointing out that, after all, Chopin's contribution to the literature of the piano was paramount, and that a pianist of eminence was in duty bound to face up to the challenge. Next year Schnabel did play Chopin in Vienna. After the recital Moritz Rosenthal went round to the artist's room. He was, even more than Rubinstein, poles apart from Schnabel. 'How did you like my Chopin?' inquired Schnabel. 'Very interesting', said Rosenthal; 'but you play it—you play Chopin different. . . .' 'Yes', replied Schnabel, 'I concentrate on the subtleties of harmony. I try to bring out the thinking, the philosophy as well as the poetry.' 'Hm', murmured Rosenthal, 'I see—Chopin-hauer.' Schnabel, who could laugh at himself, would tell this story with relish. His wit usually was sharply barbed. At a rehearsal with Georg Szell of a Beethoven concerto—the C minor, I think—there was an argument between them concerning tempi. 'But, Artur', insisted Szell, 'I have seen the original metronome markings in the original "Partitur", in Beethoven's own "Handschrift".' 'Yes', said Schnabel: 'and I have seen the original metronome. And it could *never* have been in order.'

This play of his essentially serious mind could set the keyboard dancing in his treatment of a quick movement of a Beethoven concerto. He played the Weber 'Konzertstück' with the swiftest and lightest of fingers. But he would insist that it is not the fingers that play; it is the mind, the feeling. It is wrong, of course, to remember Schnabel exclusively as a sort of Beethoven high priest who could hold us breathless even in a Beethoven pause, or silence. Like Furtwängler, he could achieve a silence which did not halt the onward course of music, a silence in which we could hear the pulse and heart of the composer beating.

He was a full man, yet with curious blind, or deaf, spots. His wife, Theresa, might go with a party in a box at the opera for *Der Rosenkavalier*, and Schnabel would politely go with them. But, as he said, 'during the performance I would surreptitiously practise the fingering of my next recital on the side of my chair.' I seldom heard him speak with fervour about any composers excepting Mozart, Beethoven, Schubert and Bach. He was anti-Wagnerian—'all sequences, no real transition. A swimmer to the next island.' Mozart was for him hardly approachable by human means of comprehension: 'always an enigma.' He told students that he preferred to play music which he considered 'to be better than it could be performed', meaning music which did not hold all its significance in the notes, its shape and so on. He *knew* that he understood everything in Chopin; not Mozart. This approach might be called extra-musical. The thinker in him shared control of his expressive technique, and of his musical receptive powers, with the artist. A Rubinstein and a Horowitz, for example, are content to be artists—artist-pianists. Not Schnabel. Purist pianists, and purist musicians, sometimes objected to Schnabel's recurrent suggestion of a didacticism.

Yet it was when the thinker took main charge of his susceptibilities that his playing became incomparable in its day for
penetration and conviction. He could never have vied, strictly
as pianist-artist, with Rubinstein, Horowitz, Godowski. His
secret as Beethoven interpreter defied analysis; at any rate,
defined my scope of analysis. It was little use attending, score
in hand, to his rhythm, to his deliberate phrasing, to the clearness of his figuration and judicious footwork on the pedals.
Many pianists, before and after Schnabel, have equalled him
in his treatment of rhythm, phrasing and so on. I felt obliged,
when listening to him in Beethoven especially, to fall back on
spiritual speculation to account for Schnabel's power to convince us, or at least to persuade us, that he was somehow going
into Beethoven's mind, nothing less, and taking us with him.
In such moments of revelatory listening, I could well believe
that Schnabel had some spiritual connection with the creative
source of Beethoven, that some fiery particles had kindled
Schnabel's being as artist and man, fiery particles sent into him
from the eternal act of musical combustion that *is* Beethoven.

During the Adagio of Op. 106 Schnabel could cause the
piano to sound as a sort of crucible in which a chemistry of the
spirit refined sound, colour, rhythm, chords and silence down
to a more remote overtoned dimension of aural appeal—visual
too, for the presence of Schnabel counted. Ideas of ultimate
substance came to my mind. I remember particularly the effect
on me of his treatment of the ornamentation which conceals the
main theme of the Op. 106 Adagio, when it returns. Also, in the
same movement, where the treble drops more than three
octaves, then rises to keyboard heights; here Schnabel would
linger, without dislocation of tempo, and evoke quite metaphysical fallings-away and vanishings. In such experiences of his
playing I, and other listeners, could reflect on the absurdity of
the notion of 'progress' in mortal comprehension or achievement. In Op. 106, played greatly yet simply (and paradoxically
Schnabel for all his mental strength and range was capable of
simplicity, or let us say, economy of expression), the mind of
man is taken as far as thought and feeling will ever reach. At
least, I can't think otherwise. As Langford wrote, we should be

proud that we belong to the same race which could produce a Beethoven, even though, we must in honesty add, we are related to Beethoven pretty much as the mud hut was related to the Parthenon.

Curiously, one of my unforgettable experiences of Schnabel was when he joined Huberman in a recital of Beethoven violin sonatas, decades ago, one Saturday afternoon in the old Queen's Hall in London, comfortable with plush, a welcoming place, the walls and plush seeming over years to have themselves absorbed music. Round the corner from the hall was the music lovers' perfect restaurant, Pagani's, always open and hospitable, Sundays, Good Fridays, Christmas Days, and there you would meet Toscanini, Kreisler, all the renowned music-makers. For the conjuration of memory I am now trying to perform, calling back into recorded life this Beethoven recital of Schnabel and Huberman, I intentionally begin from lunchtime at Pagani's on a November Saturday; intimacy in a world not long to survive, a civilisation dead now as the dodo. It was all a dream, in a London retaining special kinds of human breeding, 'the drawing-room of civilised men and women', to drag in the phrase of the forgotten George Meredith. Not a drawing-room altogether. The Queen's Hall had its servants' entrance; but the servants took on a reflection in appearance and manner. The class distinctions had not yet been exposed as the terrible social evil and injustice that none of us, not even the kitchen-maid, suspected that they then were. Into the stream of my consciousness come and go these impressions. Pagani's, destroyed by German bombs, the Queen's Hall destroyed by German bombs, Schnabel dead, Huberman dead, the 1930s dead, the 1970s, I suppose, alive, America on the moon—yet in my consciousness, this recital of Schnabel and Huberman is vitally with me, almost visually, the cosy scene, the hushed Queen's Hall, the twilight beginning to cover London, the stately and quiet Portland Place; the scene, the setting, immediate and adjacent, loom in my memory. I am there again. The flash-backs of time . . . mysterious, hallowed, cherishable.

Before the event, it would have been a pretty safe conjecture that Huberman and Schnabel were not artists exactly suggesting by their style and temperament a wedding of true minds. But it is error to suppose that like turns to like in this world (hence the general persistence of more or less blissful states of matrimony). The conjunction of Huberman and Schnabel in a musical performance made Hegelians of us (for the time being; for the time being only—fortunately for us), believing in the identity of opposites, in the truth that emerges when a positive has discovered its natural and logical negative. We know, have known for years, the characteristics of Schnabel in Beethoven; we know and have always known exactly what he lacked because of the sway of those characteristics. Huberman possessed that something which Schnabel had not; and his own temperamental and technical loose ends were corrected by Schnabel. It was, as they played Beethoven together, a case of outline and logic receiving colour and nervous sensibility; and of colour and nervous sensibility receiving outline and logic. Huberman's tendency, as violinist, was towards a subtly plastic nuance of melody and rhythm; Schnabel's tendency was towards direct, unequivocal statement—the essentials, no more, no less. When these two great musicians, who happened each to be a great man, were playing together, we were given almost the ideal synthesis.

The sonatas performed on this afternoon of lasting time conjuration were, I am sure, the second of Op. 30; certainly, the glorious one in G major. Usually we hear a violin sonata rather lop-sidedly, so to say; violin or piano too prominent. Schnabel and Huberman found the same scale of tone on the whole, though no pianist, alive or dead, could hope to match a percussive instrument to the gutty softness of Huberman's fiddle during quiet passages. Huberman presented us with the romance and bloom of Beethoven, just as Schnabel gave us the wisdom and humanity. This dual playing brought home unforgettably the range of Beethoven's nature and art; everything was here— imagination and fancy, muscle and grey matter, invention and creation, matter and spirit. Everything that is, save geniality. Huberman was short of simple humour (*not* Schnabel!). He had an impish caprice but not the unbuttoned laugh. Huberman was, at one and the same time, a romantic and a classic, gipsy and, like Schnabel, serious searcher after the thing-in-itself. Neither performed to a public. The audience attended as though to overhear a communion of rare spirits. Gone—as the gentleman in Dickens lamented—perfectly gone!

Elena Gerhardt

Elena Gerhardt seems to be forgotten. Sixty years ago she was known and accepted everywhere as the Muse of Lieder. As far as this country is concerned, she made Lieder a rare possession of our musical culture up and down the land, from London to what was then called 'the provinces'. Until her advent, a concert wholly devoted to Lieder was out of the common market of Britain's concert traffic and economy. Vocalists then appearing solo often sang adorned in white gloves if they were male, black if they were women, presenting to us a repertory of opera arias (piano accompaniment) followed, to relieve our withered emotions, by a drawing-room ballad by Guy d'Hardelot or Tosti. Clara Butt, having resonantly sung Gluck at us, once came down the floral-resplendent platform and, in deep tones, and as capacious as a battleship, informed the audience that she would, as an encore, sing 'Dear little jammy-face'.

Gerhardt, occasionally with Nikisch playing the piano for her, sometimes with the uniquely gifted Ivor Newton as accompanist, interpreted Schubert as never before in my experience, and as never since. Her voice was the instrument of an inbred style, a voice of unflaked marble, as she sang Schubert's 'Die Allmacht' with an unforgettable dignity and power. The mighty apostrophe at the beginning was nobly directed; the opening phrase and the transition to tenderness came to us like a poignant condescension. There was the softest heart-easing caress in the vocal turn to the word 'erbarmen'. In this song, 'Die Allmacht', we could feel that if Gerhardt had not given herself entirely to Lieder she might have become one of the greatest or most poetically and musically convincing artists in music-drama—a Kundry or an Erda, even if the score had to suffer some transition of key. Before she intoned a note she established the mood of a song. Her poise, deportment and facial expression were right and, so to say, consummated in advance of all the music which was to come. For 'Die Allmacht' the face seemed as a mask hiding familiar mortality. Then—*mirabile dictu*—in 'Auf dem Wasser zu singen' we were put into touch with an essentially *gemütlich* Elena; the *woman* in her rippled with delight in the music; the music rippled invisibly over the whole of her; and she was full-blown of stature. Her voice in this song was the beating pulse of pleasure. Her transitions had such subtlety that there was no risk of the merely picturesque or imitative. As a fact, her voice was quite economical in its use of shading and colour; the transitions, the imaginative metamorphoses were achieved psychologically, by an enveloping mood, a mental projection to the heart of the song; not the consequence of drawing upon reach-me-down 'characterization' tricks of the vocalist's trade. Her interpretations were seldom realistic to the point of disillusion; song from Gerhardt was unflawed and un-stressed by the burdens of an extraneous verbal expression. Her art placed emotion in a sort of glass, wherein poignancy lost starkness of edge, but was seen to be even more poignant because it was now more than real—it was just fine art and beautiful. As simple and conclusive as that.

She found close touch with perfection within limitations. Wolf at his most subtle eluded her; she could not convey the dawn-mystery of, say, 'Geh' Geliebte', or the ache of 'Sehn-sucht' in 'Kennst du das Land'. Even the Strauss setting of 'Schlechtes Wetter' lacked the Heine tincture when Gerhardt sang. To say the truth, Strauss himself does not provide the right acidity and tell us the half of Heine's picture and implied comment; the terrible weather; the old mother braving the hail to buy comforts for her daughter ('für's grosse Töchter-lein'), who sits at home, warm and lazy, apparently enjoying reasons of her own for not having to worry about the weather, or the next meal, or the meal after. Gerhardt could not approach the bitter-sweet, the inimical, the uncomfortable. Her good nature made her the ideal Schubert interpreter.

There are rare times in a life when we look upon a lovely artist knowing in our hearts that we are sharing an experience not likely ever to come our way again in this guise. Pavlova caused me to feel this sense of a precious unique delight; Ellen Terry and Kathleen Ferrier stirred the same sense of unflaunted beauty passing by us, touched with mortality and therefore to be guarded over jealously; though, as a fact, Gerhardt's art and presence had an embracing substantiality which hardly encouraged mortality to cross her path at all.

Menuhin

When Yehudi Menuhin, a boy of some fifteen years, played the solo part of the Elgar Violin Concerto in the Royal Albert Hall in 1932, the composer conducting, everybody present, with intelligent ears to hear, became aware that this was a fiddler blessed with a tone as much born from the instrument's mellowed wood as Kreisler's, a tone shaped into musical phrases, risings and fallings, by a bow and by fingers directed by genius already mature. Myself, I asked: 'What will he be able to do in the future? He can never add to, or develop, these perfectly presented violin attributes.' Such was the aesthetic problem Menuhin soon was obliged to try to solve. The tyranny of a tone, a fulfilled unchanging violin language, can get in the way of freedom of interpretation. Young Yehudi stained all composers with the same sense-rapturing dyes; he caused the second subject of the first movement of the Elgar Violin Concerto to sound as though affined to Max Bruch. The Chaconne of Bach, played by this 'Wunderkind', entirely engaged the sensuous susceptibilities of the listener; a classic austerity, or any musical characteristic not ordered by the dominating persuasiveness of young Yehudi's violin, was kept at a certain distance. Huberman, who as a fiddler did not at any time of his career command Yehudi's tone and control of it, decided for a while to break away from his instrument's dictatorship, and study philosophy at the Sorbonne. In the autumn of 1939, when Hitler marched into action, I heard Menuhin playing at a concert in Manchester at the beginning of the tense 'phoney' war, the period of dread expectation, the first black-outs; the feeling among most of us was helpless inactivity, while the twilight of our civilisation descended everywhere. In a Manchester cinema, Menuhin played, with a pianist named Endt, the G major Violin Sonata of Brahms. He was now in his mid-twenties; experience had lost no time liberating his art from the thrall of his violin's allurements. His tone was here visited by a spiritualised sensuousness; the necessary metamorphosis was happening, transforming the prodigy to the musical thinker known to the world today.

A year or so following this performance of the G major Sonata in a Manchester cinema, I came personally to know Yehudi. I first spoke to him in Sydney, near my flat, adjoining the cosmopolitan King's Cross. The war was going Hitler's way; Yehudi had grown almost beyond the reach of music as an art in itself. He was seeking for a wider, more humanly pragmatic means of communication. 'I played the violin as well as I'll ever play it when I was in my teens', he told me. His mind and spirit, aching for devotion to a shattered world's needs, rebelled against the restrictions of a solo concert performer's routine. The thought struck me, as he talked on an Australian afternoon blazing away in sunshine which should surely have filled and pacified the whole universe, that here was a much more than marvellously gifted young violinist; this was a great man, maturing day by day—he could inspire people, lead them, as priest, statesman, philosopher. He spoke of a desire for wider horizons. Music, of course, must always be his way of life, his way of social and ethical world-betterment. Through the medium of his fiddle, he hoped to root out deeper significances than those contained in the notes written down in black and white during a composer's lifetime.

A violin for Menuhin is now what a pen is to a poet, or a brush to a painter; it is for him a means to an end. Sooner or later, every masterful technician in the arts comes face to face with the problem which the young Menuhin was called on to tackle. Can he ever escape from his own born craftsmanship and become an artist who can re-create? The problem has stiffened during the last decade or two. In the most scientific and mechanical age known throughout civilised history, music has become a part of the background of the increasingly technological *rationale*. Personal impulse is suspect and likely to fall under the suspicion of being 'romantic'. The ear accustomed to the gramophone demands accuracy, strait-jacketed fidelity to the printed notes.

I am deliberately simplifying this problem of technique-contra-aesthetic freedom. Even the 'scientific' music critic, the latter-day score-vigilant Beckmessers, are not likely to make too much of technical accuracy if there is nothing else accompanying it—some fundamental brainwork. But temperament and improvisation are asking for trouble, nonetheless. Menuhin in his maturity, as man and violinist, is subject to constant complaints from critics because of his 'insecure intonation'. I should have thought that if a mature and experienced artist is going through technical ups-and-downs it is obvious enough that the technical vagaries are not the consequence of carelessness or faltering fingers or failing ears. It would not be a good sign if a Heifetz, or an Isaac Stern, were to vacillate in technical controls. (Here, I hasten to add that I am not suggesting that a Heifetz, or a Stern, is under an iron necessity to play technically well because he has nothing but technique to give us.) But in their different styles, Heifetz and Stern have contented themselves with fidelity to their medium, contented themselves with the art of glorifying and ennobling the violin. Menuhin is a musical seeker in the way that Schnabel and Busoni were, and as Arrau and Klemperer are today. We tend to forget that though Menuhin, as I write these lines, is, as great men and musicians go, still a young man of some few more than fifty years, he was, all the same, nurtured in a nineteenth-century musical aesthetic, very much steeped in extra-musical associations, supposedly spiritual or ethical. The Menuhin breed, the Klemperer breed, are getting rarer and rarer.

Music was regarded by Busoni as something of a mystery, in which only those prepared for dedication should ever actively participate. Music is now mainly regarded as a contribution to public entertainment. A public, unlike any known anywhere half a century ago, attends concerts, a public which is rather more gramophonic or televisionary than it is musical. Into this epoch of democratic musical sharing, Menuhin has gone his soul-destined way. To arrive at a state of dedication which did not fetter self-exploration, Menuhin was obliged to submit to a psychological change endangering such superficialities as 'exact intonation'. He surrendered, so to say, his skill to the service of ever-transitory creative music, music with what the forgotten metaphysician, Samuel Alexander, called 'imputations'. Not all the significance of Beethoven is in the notes, heard as notes pure and intoned with rectitude. A Menuhin performance is endowed with the life, nerve and the pulsating, always questioning intelligence of the man himself, as he stands there on the platform before us, sometimes seeming to reincarnate Mozart, or some other visitant from a more finely-grained, more spiritually charged world than this. He never *performs*; he communicates to us, through his fiddle, often in spite of his fiddle, the divinely given best of him. And I use the word 'divinely' with deliberation. In Claridges one day at lunch, the head waiter came to Yehudi's table with an apt greeting: 'Mr. Menuhin, how are you—fit as a fiddle?' He is more than that. Once the slave, the enchanted young slave, spell-bound by sounds coming as though uncalled from inside the mellow wood of his instrument, he is now the violin's master, free to get out of tune with it, if needs be.

MILADY

I met her by sheer chance. In the summer of 1928 I was writing about music and cricket stationed in Manchester. Nearly every week I went to London to cover a concert there, or a match at Lord's or at the Oval. During the Canterbury cricket Festival of that year, when I was coping with Lancashire and Yorkshire at Old Trafford, a letter came to me, my first from her. It was written in pencil on a page torn out of a notebook. It informed me that she had strained an ankle and was 'lying prone' in bed, unable to go to Canterbury to see Woolley batting. The letter was posted in a Kent town, where she lived. 'You', she wrote, 'will surely understand the deprivation I am undergoing.' I couldn't ignore the tone, the charm of the letter, so I replied suggesting that one day we might meet.

A month or two later I had to go to London for a Kreisler recital. We arranged, by post, to meet at the bookstall in Charing Cross station. We described roughly our individual appearances. On October 8, 1928, I positioned myself at the rendezvous. For ten minutes I waited; no sign of anybody answering to her self-identification. Then, as I was about impatiently to depart, she emerged from the ladies waiting-room where she had been, as she put it, 'carefully inspecting me'. Frankly I was disappointed by her appearance and dress; she looked pale, and might well have been the next suburban office-girl.

We walked from the station across Trafalgar Square; and while we were dodging the traffic she asked me if I would lend her ten shillings. She had laddered her stocking, and had come out forgetting her purse. I gave her a ten-shilling note while we were having coffee in a café in the Haymarket. After an hour's more or less conventional talk I told her that I had to leave for an appointment elsewhere, which wasn't true. I could have taken her to lunch, spent the whole day with her, dinner and a theatre in the evening. I got rid of her on the pavement opposite His Majesty's Theatre, where I picked up a taxi. I asked her if I could give her a lift anywhere. She said: 'No, thank you. Goodbye.' Before the afternoon was over, no stronger notion of her remained with me than of a pleasant young woman with beautiful eyes and a large generous mouth.

Next day, or the day after, she sent me a ten-shilling note and a letter of one sentence: 'I really did leave my purse at home.' A month later I met her again; I hadn't the heart to let her think that one look at her had been enough for me. I arranged to take her to dinner one Saturday in the Howard Hotel, near the Embankment. I waited for her in the lounge. She came through the swing-door to the minute. In my dying hour I shall remember the radiance which now emanated from her. Her eyes were more lustrous (and alluring) than any I had ever before seen. Her high cheekbones were vivid, her natural colours. Her lips were rose red, also by the dowry of nature. She walked with a suggestion of a swaying side-way motion. This time she was simply but charmingly dressed; a small grey hat which followed the shape of the back of her head, her hair coiled in wheels about her ears. When she uncoiled her hair for me—but not yet!—it fell to her knees. She was thin, or rather, slender, not too tall. Her head fitted perfectly into my shoulder. When I took her arm to lead her to the restaurant I felt the life in her trembling. I had known this sensation only once before, when I had a bird in my hand. At dinner she talked as if she had known me for years. I asked her why at our first meeting she had looked so different. 'Engine troubles', she replied.

She burned a flame of sex and being. She had found my wavelength; and it was a flame blown about fitfully now and then. Between her eyes a line would sometimes appear, a straight thin wrinkle. I guessed she had gone through some troubles, not to say endangering experiences, one time or other. She sensed what was passing through my mind and in a low voice, her chin resting on her hands, said: 'Yes, I have been naughty, but I was educated in a convent in France and always help with the harvest festival at our church.'

I do her no wrong, this wonderful girl, if I write that whenever I introduced her to anybody redolent of English middle-class flavours I could stand aside to note their reactions to her. I could almost hear them asking themselves: 'Who—what is she *really*?' But abroad, in Germany and Austria, men such as Huberman, Schnabel, Stefan Zweig, Arnold Rosé and Weingartner at once fell under her spell. She could, as she would say, 'produce' herself, given the occasion. In London she was admired by Sir Thomas Beecham; and C. B. Fry invariably addressed her as 'Milady'.

We were together in Salzburg during the Festival of 1932. Deep in conversation we crossed the road near the Stein Hotel, failing to take notice of a prohibitive sign to pedestrians. A policeman charged after us, crying out officiously: 'Durchfahrt verboten!' With a regal toss of her head she said to him: 'Durchfahrt yourself!'—and we proceeded on our way. At Salzburg this same year, if I remember well, Anton Weiss of the Vienna Philharmonic Orchestra insisted we should go on to Vienna at the end of the Festival to hear Weingartner conducting *The Ring*. Weiss assured us that he would give instructions at the secretary's office of the Staatsoper that tickets would be waiting for us, reserved seats for the performance of *Das Rheingold*.

So, to Vienna we journeyed; and on a golden September afternoon I entered the secretary's office at the Opera to pick up the promised tickets, leaving my beauteous one waiting on the pavement outside. But there were no tickets for us, no seats reserved; the performance was 'ausverkauft'—sold out. I protested—'But Herr Weiss promised.' No avail; there had been a mistake. I departed from the office and, outside, told her about it all. 'It doesn't matter', I said, 'I don't particularly want to hear *Rheingold*. I'd much rather we went to Hartmann's for dinner.' She expostulated. (And how she *could* expostulate, eyes and mouth.) 'But I'd like very much to hear *Rheingold* in Vienna.

Besides, we were promised. *I'll* go and see to it.' Through the imposing doors she walked, in spite of my protestations that it would be useless for her to argue.

For nearly an hour I stood in the street; opposite was a jeweller's shop bearing the name of 'Hugo Wolf'. I paced up and down. I furtively peeped into the corridor leading to the secretary's office in the Staatsoper. No sign of her. Then she reappeared, holding in her hand a card of admission that evening to the Director's box—*du lieber Himmel*, to the Director's *private* box! 'Good God', I exclaimed, 'but how—how did you get this?' 'I persuaded them to lead me to Dr. Weingartner', she said. 'And', said I, 'what then?' 'I was NICE to him', she replied. And I find it necessary, for the purposes of true and living communication, to have the word 'nice' printed in capital letters.

We proceeded that evening to the Director's box, armed with our imperative card of admission. When we arrived at the box, it was crowded—crowded with civil servants, hangers-on of the Staatsoper staff. They were all cleared out, every one of them, and we sat there alone throughout the performance. Opera glasses in plenty digressed from the stage to look at her. Next day the Vienna press printed inquisitive paragraphs about 'die schöne Engländerin'. After this *Rheingold* performance we went to Hartmann's restaurant, and soon Weingartner himself entered, straight from the conductor's desk, accompanied by one or two famous singers. He was wearing a long crimson-lined cape, and before divesting himself of it and seating himself with his guests, came to our table. He took her hand, kissed it, and with accent and intonation of an aristocrat, hoped she had enjoyed the performance. Then he kissed her hand again, clicked his heels, bowed to her, and departed to his own table, taking not the slightest notice of me.

There was no artificiality about her. When she projected herself it was not done to impress others but to get the best out of herself in a given situation or scene. I would watch her when she wasn't aware that I was watching. Like a young girl she would review herself in front of a wardrobe mirror, swirling around, showing herself to herself. She pretended to no wide culture;

and whenever she was with those who knew their subject, she was discretion itself. But she was a good and careful reader, with so sure an instinct for the best music, poetry and literature that often, while formally educated people were talking nonsense, I could feel that, as she quietly listened, she was thinking devastating sense. At a supper dominated by Sir Thomas Beecham, he began really to talk nonsense about conductors. 'Toscanini is generally known to be short-sighted, hence his necessity to pretend independence of a score as he conducts.' And so on, until Sir Thomas turned his tongue and attention ridiculously on Bruno Walter. 'Sloppy. No control.' And soft of voice and looking Sir Thomas straight into his eyes with her glorious own, she simply murmured: 'Balls, Sir Thomas.' Sir Thomas was enchanted.

She never ceased to surprise me by her contrasts of extrovert enjoyment followed by abrupt transitions to a quite self-indulgent seriousness. She could achieve a crisis which would ruin a day out with her. If she caught a chill she at once wanted her temperature taken. A tight shoe would put an end to a walk in the country almost before we had gone a hundred yards. The irony of these imagined maladies is that she was victim of a most cruel asthma which at night would overwhelm her until she terrified me by her gaspings for breath. She never suffered this way in my presence; she would go into another room, assuring me that the affliction was not dangerous, just something she had to go through, like the 'curse' every month. In an adjoining room she would burn some medicinal paper, inhale the fumes, and wait patiently for the paroxysm to pass. Next morning she was as fresh with bloom of life as ever.

At the height of a riot of an enjoyment of herself, with a laughter which, in an English restaurant, often provoked surprised glances towards our table, she would make a decrescendo worthy of Furtwängler himself and ask: 'Do you think *Hamlet* really is two plays patched together?' If I affected to exhibit on any subject a more expert knowledge than truly I possessed— and to tease her I sometimes did so pretend—she would say: 'That'll do, my dear: save it for Sir Thomas.' Always she told me to save my blarney for Sir Thomas. As I say, she was not a systematic reader, but had the gift to get to the core of a book as though intuitively. Her sense of words was gorgeous. She savoured them on her red tongue, licked them with her red lips.

One week-end we stayed at a sort of temperance hotel in Southend-on-Sea; I cannot think why. It was mainly occupied by maiden ladies of certain age. With a show of respectability we had booked separate bedrooms. Towards midnight I stole along the corridor, dressing-gown and pyjamas, to join her. Arrived in her room I suddenly realised I needed to spend a penny. I was not prepared to creep again along the corridor to the lavatory, disturbing the maiden ladies or exciting them. A night commode reposed in the corner of her bedroom. I opened its door, used the pot, and then washed myself. So eager was I to go to her as she lay in her bed like a queen of love that I ran to her forgetting to return the pot to the commode. She interrupted my ecstatic flight to her with: 'Do you propose to leave that vessel there all night?' *Vessel!* A common utilitarian word exalted from its habitual context and given, for me, an immortality of full-mouthed humour. 'Do you propose?'—and 'vessel'! Her mind could move with the wing of wit. One Sunday after lunch at Pagani's restaurant we were travelling in a taxi. Out of a side-street another car, speeding recklessly, hit our taxi amidship, hurtling it and us and the driver over on its side with a horrible crash, splintering glass and all to the pavement. Marvellously, none of us was hurt. I took her to my arms. 'My God', I said, 'we might both have been killed.' 'Yes', she replied, 'and the wrong way up.'

She had no time for primness in talk or in writing; she went so far as to cast Ernest Newman out of her court, much as she admired him as critic, because he persistently used the word 'commence'. She knew much of Shakespeare by heart, revelled in Dickens, delighted to read from Rabelais, especially his account of the pleasure he got from wiping his bottom, after evacuation, with the soft feathers of a goose's neck. She would chortle at the Sitwells—'all dutifully writing every morning in their different apartments, like a sort of literary sewing-guild'.

For two years of the seven I knew her we went about together all over England and abroad, to Salzburg, Vienna and Paris; and though we shared the same bed during this period I remained virginal. She would lie with her head on my left shoulder. I would kiss her, brush her lips gently. That she was able so long to discipline her nature this way was sublime. I was not, I think, even unwittingly cruel to her. My way of consummating our love may well have tormented most women of her fully-charged sexuality. She found a spiritual pride in it all. For me, for two years, it was her beauty, her nature, her *being*, that seduced my mind and senses. The sweetness of her breath alone was a seduction. And it was not an evening spent listening to *Tristan und Isolde* or any other stimulus to sexual desire which was the cause of my awakening. We had heard at the Queen's Hall the Seventh Symphony of Sibelius—least erotic music extant. At the concert's end she went to bed in the hotel where we were staying—separate rooms. I had to go to Fleet Street to write my review. After writing it I walked back to the hotel on a warm September night. I paced up and down Villiers Street. It was, fittingly, in the Charing Cross Hotel that I first went into her; the same Charing Cross Hotel where at the station bookstall I had met her, and nearly lost her, in a day. Into her room I came in pyjamas and closed the door. As I lay with her and saw in her eyes the light of the full glow and meridian of love, she said in her low, secret, yet adoringly laughing voice: 'My dear, *festina lente!*'

One morning, years after this my awakening, at the height of our high summer of communion, we went one autumn day to Windsor for an outing. We were walking along a narrow street, and I stopped to look into the window of a bookshop, while she went a few paces ahead. Then, suddenly, I saw her objectively: I was often trying to look at her with detachment. Now, on this autumn morning of ripe sunshine, I saw her as though anew. She was wearing a scarf loosely tied. I looked at her like a painter inspecting a canvas, brush in hand. And I flew to her, embraced her, kissed her. She received the kiss with the whole of her indulgent mouth. And, at this crucial moment, a line of small Eton boys came round the corner and saw us. 'My God!' I exclaimed, 'what an example we have given them.

So young and innocent.' And she said: 'Let them begin with the classics.'

At a theatre or a concert she was the perfect companion, never saying the wrong thing. During a performance of *Tristan und Isolde* she would have tears dropping down her cheeks when Kurwenal died. In the interval of the same performance she would be saying, 'Oh, these bloody shoulder-straps.' When she was present at Noël Coward's *Bitter Sweet* (or whatever it was) and the hero was suddenly shot or stabbed, she cried out from her seat in the stalls, so that the entire audience around her could hear: 'Crikey!'

She was Eliza Doolittle before and after Professor Higgins had taken her in hand. But I never grew accustomed to her face. It constantly changed, responsive to her volatile mind and temperament. Even in her sleep her face didn't have repose. She was alive in her dreams, 'producing' them, herself the principal and endearing character. In my last moments of this life I shall hope to hear her reading, *not* reciting:

> Go not, happy day,
> From the shining fields,
> Go not, happy day,
> Till the maiden yields.
> Rosy is the West,
> Rosy is the South,
> Roses are her cheeks,
> And a rose her mouth.

All in a tone soft and as beautifully modulated as the viola of Lionel Tertis. Life in her was too abundant and self-consuming. It couldn't last. She died, suddenly, still young, a rare gift to the gods, rare and premature.

. VIENNA MEMORIES

To Lili

Noch einmal Wien !

Vienna at Christmas 1924, the Ringstrasse walled high with masonically piled-up snow. The statue of Goethe presented him towelled as though for a shave. I have seen men and women, even children, make an obsequie to this statue of Goethe; if he is read at all nowadays he is taken for granted as one of the out-of-date All-Father sages of his period; and the wonder grows that the man who could regard it worth his while to function in the petty councils of Weimar had it in him to conceive and produce to the world Mephisto. As I contemplated Goethe in the snow in Vienna in 1924, I, like many of his neophytes then, did not know the half of him. I certainly did not know—and I have met few of his most devoted readers who do know—of the 'Tagebuch', the *Diary*, telling of Goethe's night at an inn. The axle of his carriage broke, so while the wheelwright was repairing it, he put up at the Star. During any journey, while away a long time from his lady—'von meiner Trauten lange Zeit entfernt'—he had thought only of her and, at nightfall, written of her in his *Diary*:

> 'Und was ich auch gewonnen und gelernet,
> So hat ich doch nur immer Sie im Sinne;
> Und wie zu Nacht der Himmel erst sich sternet,
> Erinn'rung uns umleuchtet ferner Minne
> So ward im Federzug des Tags Ereignis
> Mit süssen Worten ihr ein freundlich Gleichnis.'

Which, freely translated, runs: 'Throughout the daily round, my thoughts were only of her; and as the first stars appeared in the night sky, the light of absent love shone round about us. Her dear reflection sweetly lay in each recorded syllable of that day's happening.'

At the Star, though, comfortable and homely, a waiting-girl came with the candle to his chamber—'Ein Mädchen kam, des seltensten Gebildes', rarely shaped. But he sat down to his portfolio, intending to record for his beloved and himself the events of the day. Somehow the words would not spread themselves. The girl came into his room again, now laden with supper. She carves the chicken neatly with graceful movements. He is captivated, leaps to his feet, seizes her. She whispers 'Hush', tells him her aunt is listening, the aged hostess in the next chamber, a Dragon. But, she softly says, 'leave your door open, stay awake, and perhaps at midnight I will come'.

A wide bed has been made for him, 'wovon den kleinsten Teil mir anzumessen, die Liebe rät'. She comes at midnight; he takes her into his arms, 'sie senkt sich her, die Wohlgestalt ergreif ich'. She is insistent that he should know that she is usually timid—'blöde'—that she has resisted the advances of men and is known for her coldness, 'stets gegen Männer setzt ich mich zur Wehre'. She loved him at sight. He is the first to have her. 'Du hast mich rein.' Then, marvellously, he is in a wondrous plight; 'so war ich doch in wunderbarer Lage'. For that part of him which at other times would rise masterfully, shrinks back . . .

> 'Denn der so hitzig sonst den Meister spielet,
> Weicht schülerhaft zurück und abgekühlet.'

She is free of her body, in rapturous consent. Yet though he lies with her, relying on his Master Tool and Executant (my translation for Goethe's 'Meister Iste') he could do nothing to her virginity. As he lay there, his desire aflame and his organ of fornication inert, he recollected that when he married his true beloved, in the presence of the priest and the altar, before Christ's cross of sorrow, 'es regte sich der Iste', his 'cock', or John Thomas, was stirring and rising. There it is, he thinks philosophically, and as at dawn the servant-maid wakes, realises the situation, and leaves him—eyes cast down—he consoles himself with the thought that his love for his only love has won against his casual urges. There it is:

> 'Doch Meister Iste hat nun seine Grillen,
> Und lässt sich nicht befehlen, noch verachten.
> Auf einmal ist er da, und ganz im stillen
> Erhebt er sich zu allen seinen Prachten.'

To translate would be to ruin the most human and humorous lines in all Goethe. As they remarkably came back to my memory, after years in oblivion, when I was looking at the snow-draped Goethe on the Ringstrasse in Vienna, this thought occurred to me as commentary: the sculptor no doubt hoped to shape and present the Sage meditating profoundly on his Theory of Colours, or on his Theory of the Metamorphosis of Plants; more likely, I inferred, from a glance in the eyes of the marble, a light thrown, like a prompter of nature—I inferred he was remembering that night in the inn, where Iste, or Jimmy, or whatever his name, was true and, really, morally responsible.

*   *   *   *   *

This is the way I look at Vienna, or any other place. I wait on a scene, a place, an atmosphere, to collaborate with my radar of sensibility. I cannot, certainly cannot, go forth to look at a view, a predetermined excursion, planned and instructed. I must be free to turn this way or that, free to live and see and insinuate myself improvisatorially into the surrounding environment; visual, historical, sensory, emotional. It is best also to go about the world alone, or with a mind-and-soul mate. No need then for adjustments of mood, movement or comment. I am selfish, no doubt, or self-centred. Yet, given the right wavelength to find the core of a companion, I can join in a wedlock of shared consciousness and awareness. And I have been lucky. In Vienna, at much the same time in history that Milady charmed Weingartner into presenting us with his Director's box at the Staatsoper, we went to the Krantz-Ambassador Hotel to dinner and there, sitting alone, was Franz Lehár, white hair, distinguished. Since my teens I had liked his music, listened to in Manchester by medium of bands in the parks; also

I had seen and heard Lily Elsie in *The Merry Widow*; and later, in the Theater an der Wien, I had seen and heard the original Hanna, Mizzi Günther. To meet Lehár now, in this restaurant of the Krantz-Ambassador, was an opportunity not to be missed. I took courage, left Milady at our table, walked over to his, and introduced myself with a sincere genuflexion. He was Viennese charm in apotheosis. He, too, genuflected. But, before inviting me to sit down with him at his table, he cast an experienced eye over to Milady and said to me: 'Bringen Sie, bitte, die Dame. . . .' He, too, was not missing an opportunity.

I prompted him to speak of his experiences in London, when he came from Vienna to attend the first performance in England of *The Merry Widow*. Whereby hangs a tale of some typical English comedy, a tale much of the English ways of the musical comedy, of the period. I can well believe that Lehár, as he sat in his box at Daly's, wondered from time to time if he had got into the right theatre. 'Wo ist meine Musik?' he might well have asked during long periods of the action taken over by George Graves, playing the role supposedly of the Baron Mirko Zeta. This name was rejected by the Daly's censors (George Edwardes and others) as too much for English tastes, so it was changed to the unmistakably comic Baron Popoff. In the original operetta, the Baron is ambassador of the little State anxious not to lose the fortune of the heroine, through marriage, to another State. George Graves was compact entirely, flesh and everything, of the London man-about-town of the nineteen-hundreds, with a brandy-and-soda breath and raffishness, senile but active in all the masculine cylinders. His horse-laugh has probably been excelled in tone and aroma only by Pyke and Pluck, the sycophants of Lord Frederick Verisopht. But there was nothing of the sycophant about Graves; his leer was enough to engage the interest of Rabelais.

In the garden scene in the *Widow*, after the lovers had retired to the little pavilion and the *dénouement* of the play was on tip-toe, Graves held up the proceedings, including the music, and any evidence to be inferred in the theatre that an orchestra was on the premises at all. For at least half an hour, Graves stole the show. He appeared in the scene accompanied by his secretary

Kisch (also a name not to be found in the original libretto). Kisch remarked admiringly on the sunset which came rosily over the stage. 'Bee-yootiful!' said Graves hoarsely, 'just like a blood-shot eye.' Then apropos of nothing, before or after, he plunged and spluttered into his famous epic of Daniel the Drake and Hetty the Hen. I forget the details; Daniel, a Hungarian duck, fell in love with the Austrian Hetty. Passion consuming him one day he came, in the language of Graves, 'dashing over the frontier' in pursuit of Hetty the hen, who, narrated Graves irrelevantly, ate some brass filings accidentally mixed-up in her food and next morning, after passionate communication from Daniel, laid a door-knob. Whether this anti-climactic end was supposed to have symbolical or even Freudian significance, or if it were merely for Graves a *non sequitur*, remained a matter for conjecture. Graves constantly broke the continuity, as he told the story, by abrupt interruptions and ejaculations, such as: 'Wait a minute—m'plate's slipped!'

No laughter in any theatre anywhere has been so uncontrolled as Graves horse-coughed this improbable and, on paper, not funny episode in the life of Daniel the Drake. His acting was a masterpiece of English coarseness and grotesque imagination, Hogarth rendered rakishly Edwardian. Baron Popoff, of course, had nothing to do with *The Merry Widow*, which in Vienna was a production of aristocratic (or at least, bourgeois) carriage and charm. 'Wo ist meine Musik?' Where indeed? There was, of course, Lily Elsie's widow, remembered affectionately by Lehár in the Krantz-Ambassador decades after; but there was not a hint of the Viennese gentle flavour of eroticism. 'Light opera' (or 'musicals' as we call them here), must, in England, contain some correction to sentiment, and to the decorative amours. Even comedy in Mozart is directed towards the farcical in England. Ochs, in *Der Rosenkavalier*, if an English artist is playing the part, is figured as rather a bucolic buffoon, related to Tony Lumpkin.

At Daly's, the waltz was, as they used to say, 'plugged' repeatedly. If my memory is sure, the waltz was heard only once or twice in the Theater an der Wien production; first in the scene where Hanna is teased by Danilo to the dance; and at

81

the end of the operetta, when she realises that he truly loves her. And the waltz was played in Vienna at a slow tempo, in the closing revelatory scene. Given this way, it was, on the lower plane of operetta, as much in character and as musically apt and expressive and *final* as the trio of *Der Rosenkavalier*.

As Lehár himself said, without false modesty, no ordinary 'musical comedy' voice can sing his music. A real, trained voice is needed to give us the light touch—with its romantic, even erotic implications—of Lehár at his best. His appeal is to the world of civilized sensualism, and to a pre-1970 notion of sexual allure. No English composer has written anything like a Lehár waltz; Noël Coward, of English composers, has come closest to achieving a waltz that pulls at the heartstrings with the faintly banal seductiveness of Lehár, Fall and Oscar Straus*. If Sullivan composed a convincing waltz at all (and he is our only composer of operetta in the same gallery as Lehár), it is like the waltz in the *Di Ballo* Overture, brilliant rather than seductive. Lehár's music is, I should say, Johann Strauss flavoured with 'Kitsch', an untranslatable term, meaning, broadly, tunes and rhythms almost cheaply familiar, yet related to music proper. I refuse to drag in the word 'vulgarity' in any discussion of Lehár; he is never 'vulgar'. And to those loftily raised eyebrows which tower above 'Kitsch', I now quote to their edification I hope, certainly with humour to myself, a phrase from a letter of Richard Strauss to Stefan Zweig: 'Muss man 70 Jahre alt werden, um zu erkennen, dass man eigentlich zum Kitsch die meiste Begabung hat?' Which is to say in English: 'Must one live to seventy to find out that one's gifts run most naturally to Kitsch?' 'Tis true, but not always is it a pity 'tis true. A natural liking for *The Merry Widow* will do nobody harm; several musicians of my acquaintance would be the better for it. There was nothing of 'Kitsch' about Lehár, the ageing connoisseur of life and good manners whom we met in the Krantz-Ambassador Hotel in Vienna, as the sun in the city's cultural sky was slowly going down, and he asked me to bring to him Milady.

---

* But, ah! — see page 158.

Lotte Lehmann and Vienna

Round about 1935 James Agate, discussing top-class actresses, asked me to name my favourite. 'Lotte Lehmann,' I unhesitatingly answered. 'I am thinking primarily of theatre, not opera,' he snapped. 'So am I,' was my response. I need only refer to her entrance in Act I of *Die Walküre* to force home the reason for my high opinion of Lehmann purely and simply as actress. She discovered the exhausted Siegmund, and with marvellous vocal nuance murmured, 'Ein fremder Mann'; at the same time the whole woman of her, the timid lean forward of her, every pulsation of her presence, made curiosity, fear and even a prophetic hint of recognition musically and histrionically visible and omnipresent. The way she came into the scene in Act III of *Der Rosenkavalier* embodied the opera's crisis, Hofmannsthal's as well as Strauss's finest moments. In Lehmann's own words, 'out of the chaos and confusion emerges a broad flowing theme that enfolds the Marschallin, like a river of beauty'. Lehmann seemed to embrace, with her heart, body, larynx and eyes burgeoningly mingled, the gorgeous full tide of the orchestral sea.

Her Marschallin remains for me without peer, for warmth of nature, impulse and, at the pinch, a dry-eyed acceptance of fate. She did not give us an aristocratic Marschallin (any more than Strauss himself did). This was a bourgeois Marschallin, yet well-bred enough to talk to her servants without the sniff of condescension. Also Lehmann's Marschallin rather ran counter to Strauss's view that the Marschallin should be sung and acted as a woman young enough, in her early thirties, to get over in time the Octavian ache and hurt, and turn to another lover; Strauss belies this verbal notion of the Marschallin in the music by which he transfigured Hofmannsthal's creation, notably the music of the first of the Marschallin's monologues in Act I, where she hears time running out 'like sand in the hour-glass'. The essence of Strauss's music for the Marschallin is of experience saddened, but not embittered. The poignancy of the Marschallin's final 'Ja! Ja!' in Act III is rendered less touching if presented by a Marschallin with a long vista of 'affairs' before her. Moreover, Lehmann's Marschallin had the laughter which is able to savour its own ripeness; a laughter born of experience. I can hear her yet, as she realised that the visitor clamoring for entrance to her room in Act I was not, after all, her husband—a laughter combining relief *and* enjoyment of the tension.

Lehmann herself would scarcely take it as a compliment to her art if we remembered her only as she reincarnated the Marschallin. As a fact, her art was truly protean. In *Der Rosenkavalier* alone, at different periods of her career, she boxed a histrionic compass lending abounding life to Sophie and Octavian, as well as to the Marschallin. She has often, in my company, spoken modestly of her vocal technique. She had enough of technique to fulfil her mind's promptings, a mind most cunningly woven of musical and dramatic and even *visual* textures. Again my memory is visited by a flash-back over years to *Die Walküre*; the ecstasy of Sieglinde's cry as the door of Hunding's hut swung open, revealing to her and Siegmund the moonlit spring night (in a period when producers of *Die Walküre* allowed Hunding to have a door in his own home). The rapture of Lehmann's voice, the gush in her throat, caught one's breath and, indeed, caught her own breath.

I am constantly astonished to remember that when first I heard and saw Lehmann, in the Vienna Opera in January 1925, she would then be verging on her thirty-sixth year. Yet she was the personification, to eye and ear alike, of Barak's pitifully frustrated young wife, recklessly selling her shadow, her seeds of sexual plenty and fruitfulness, for the gratification of her senses and yearning and natural desire for the pleasures of the world. If I had experienced Lehmann only as the Dyer's wife,

I'd be positive about her high rank among the stage and theatre presences and powers I have known; and they range from Bernhardt, Duse, Réjane, Patrick Campbell to Jean Forbes-Robertson, Edith Evans and to Peggy Ashcroft. The production, the consummation, of Strauss's *Die Frau ohne Schatten* in Vienna at the turn of the years 1924–1925 counts among the most compellingly imaginative of all I have witnessed and participated in, senses and entire aesthetic consciousness. The producer, I think, was Roller. Barak's house was a glory of dyes, stained drapings and furniture, symbolical but nonetheless realistic in a way defeated by the *precise* realists on the one hand, and the desperate surrealists on the other. Strauss himself conducted on this unforgettable night, where I made my first acquaintance of Lehmann as artist; he had before him, on the desk, the enormous orchestral score and every page was conscientiously turned over. When I met Strauss years following this dedicatory event of my life, I asked him: 'Herr Strauss, you have often conducted *Elektra, Salome,* but seldom do you conduct *Rosenkavalier*.' He laughed. 'No—it is too difficult!' The cast for *Die Frau ohne Schatten,* on the occasion I am reliving now, was Lehmann (the Dyer's wife), Richard Mayr (Barak), Weidt (the Nurse), Oestvig (the Emperor) and Jeritza (the Empress). When *Die Frau ohne Schatten* was staged on the reopening of the Vienna Opera, in 1955, I was lunching with Hilde Güden and others of the Staatsoper company, still more or less a permanently established ensemble in Vienna. I told them of the cast I had seen and heard in 1925; and Güden and her guests in one voice exclaimed: 'Du lieber Himmel!'

The irony is that, for all the assembled talents and iridescence of personality at this marvellous realisation of *Die Frau ohne Schatten* in Vienna, half a century ago, the music-drama was, even for the more intelligent public, wherever presented, regarded as a miscarriage, a hotch-potch of fairy-story, 'instant' sex-psychology plus a post-Wagnerian Strauss. Myself, I was rather at a loss at the sight of the fish flying from the frying pan; I had not seen the libretto at my initial acquaintance with *Die Frau ohne Schatten.* I asked Arnold Rosé one morning in Hartmann's restaurant if he could tell me where I could lay hands on an English translation of Hofmannsthal's text. 'There is not yet even a translation of it into German,' he said. As simple truth, there is no incident, no imagery in *Die Frau ohne Schatten*, which a child would not at once take into his or her understanding and comprehension of super-normal beings and doings. 'Es ist mein Meisterwerk,' Strauss maintained to me. A creation of his labour is usually the most loved work of an artist. After living with *Die Frau ohne Schatten* for many years, longer than the accumulated years of many of the work's critic detractors, I am satisfied that it is just about the most deeply thoughtful commentary on life, material and spiritual, to be found in any opera composed since *Fidelio*. I thank Lehmann for taking me, by her penetration, into the quiddity of the words and music, taking me with her, through trial and error, to the core.

Strauss wrote of *Die Frau* modestly, after telling Hofmannsthal that 'you have written nothing more beautiful in your life. I am flattered that it has been brought about by our collaboration. I can only hope that my music will be worthy.' His genius short-circuited here and there, as he set the text, with its strange imagery and admixture of fairy lore and sophisticated human-all-too-human psychological drama; the end of the score is Strauss composing from memory, and by effort. All the same, Hofmannsthal led Strauss not only through a mush of half-baked Freudian imputations, but also to poignantly mortal responses, to soul questionings. He challenged not only the artist who had created the Marschallin, Oktavian, Sophie and Ochs; he called for high seriousness in Strauss, for austerity, and abstention from a bourgeois ease of looking at the world. By putting his music at the service of such characters as Barak, the Dyer's wife and the Empress, Strauss rose above his normal stature and achieved 'Verklärung'—'transfiguration'. The Empress is one of the most touchingly poetic and lovable of all opera characters. She is born of the magical overworld; and, by acquaintance with human sorrow, becomes herself, exquisitely and sufferingly human. Her music, when she first comes before us, is remotely fine-spun, with ornaments which pulsate with the nerve and sensibility of a gazelle. Awakened by contact with the sad perplexity of mortal ideals and stupidity, her music grows into human experience, and as she bows before the dread presence of the god of the overworld and as she sings, or says —'Vater bist du; hier ist dein Kind'—we hear music as much purified and ennobled by tears of trust, fear, prayerfulness and devotion, as any composed.

It rejoices me to think that Stravinsky despises Strauss. Not that I myself despise much of Stravinsky's music; in fact I was one of the publicity pioneers of 'Le Sâcre' ages ago. But Stravinsky and some of his neophytes of small stature of talent, minions of Stravinsky, who is a master at any rate, have perpetuated the lie that Strauss was a materialist, half-educated, too fond of the money bags. He was, of course, among composers in bulk from Tubal Cain to Stockhausen, one of the most cultured in literature and the arts. But he was modest about his music, would have given all of it in exchange for a little finger of Mozart's hand. He seldom belittled his colleague composers, as Stravinsky does. I am tickled at Stravinsky's comment on Bruckner: 'You can turn over fifty pages of a Bruckner score, while listening to one of his symphonies, and he is still in the same place when the music catches you up,' or words to the same effect. The joke in this statement (a joke not suspected to be there at all by Stravinsky) is that the remark applies even more aptly to the score of 'Le Sâcre du Printemps', notably to the last handful of the score's pages.

It is time we got rid of the cant about Strauss. He was honest about himself, placed himself in proper proportion to the unquestionably great:

'I fully realise that my symphonic works do not stand comparison with the giant genius of Beethoven; I know just how far my operas fall short, in grandeur of conception, originality and cultural wisdom, of Richard Wagner's monumental contribution to the art. But taking the development of the theatre as a whole, I think I am entitled to a modest conviction that when history comes to be written—and taking into account the great variety of my dramatic material and the form of its treatment—my operas will have a place of honour "at the end of the rainbow" when ranged alongside all previous theatrical works (Wagner, of course, excepted).'

Everybody agrees that Strauss composed too easily; he was the first to say it. He couldn't play 'Skat' all the time. There are passages in Strauss where I can sympathise with Stravinsky's allergy (to use a 'tenderer' word). But Strauss was without affectations. Once upon a time, he was as 'modern' as the latest (up to the moment of going to press) atonalist. He was named the 'Buddha of music', and he made a comment upon the intended compliment: 'I don't know who is the Buddha of music, but I guess who is the Pest.' I liked his show of comfortable Philistinism, refreshing after much mingling with the intellectuals. Of Bach's *St. Matthew Passion* he said: 'Matthäus Passion, vielleicht; aber nicht meine!' So say, if not all of us, at least some of us.

* * * * *

Lehmann and Vienna are not in the background of this my memory of Strauss. Lehmann was too late to incorporate into her being Madeleine of Strauss's last testament *Capriccio*. She would have absorbed the part to her inmost; for Madeleine is a sort of daughter of the Marschallin. It is easy to imagine how Lehmann would have sung, as a cry from the heart, and from the throat, Madeleine's:

> 'Nun, liebe Madeleine, was sagt dein Herz?
> Du wirst geliebt und kannst dich nicht schenken.
> Du fandest es süss, schwach zu sein.'

> *Now, dear Madeleine, what says your heart?*
> *You are loved and yet cannot return that love.*
> *You found pleasure in weakness.*

And how intently she would have intoned, holding her audience also intent, the words 'In eins verschmolzen sind Worte und Töne—zu einem Neuen verbunden. Geheimnis der Stunde . . .' The rise of Madeleine's voice on the word 'Geheimnis'— 'secret'—is inspired; I decline to name the musical interval (after the current 'analytical' banalists). There is no doubt of

Strauss's own solution to the basic problem dealt with in *Capriccio*: which is the dominant factor in opera, words or music, symbolised in the three characters. The Countess is really the Muse. Flamand and Olivier fall under her sway, and she has to decide which to take to her heart, Flamand or Olivier, music or poetry. Strauss endows Flamand with abundant melody; Olivier gets little. I regard the scene depicting Flamand in the library, declaring his love to Madeleine, the most beautiful of all Strauss's music, as an evocation of hushed throbbing twilit romance. Flamand tells Madeleine how he has watched her in the library, reading. He sat in the corner, silently watching, held his breath. 'Page after page I saw you turning. Twilight fell. When I opened my eyes you were gone. I picked up your book and read "In love silence is better than speech".' At the phrase, 'Seite um Seite sah ich Euch lesen ... Dämmerung brach herein', Strauss magically creates not only the scene and the young lover's beating breast, but, without extraneous echoes of music modes or idioms, recreates the period, remote, aristocratic, suffused with the 'pathos of distance'.

Capriccio is a harvest of ripening years. In his creation of Madeleine, Strauss gave to opera its last gracious well-bred soprano part, its last woman singing for love, and to be loved. We were unlucky never to have had the opportunity to hear Lehmann as Madeleine; we were most lucky to be granted the consolation of hearing or seeing Lisa della Casa; and of hearing on record Schwarzkopf, enveloped in the music, music almost too intangibly pulsating with love for the tough theatre of the 1970s. All of life, music and the scene and the air surrounding her passed, by the same poetic affinity, into the mind and nature of Lehmann. She was, still is, Marschallin and Madeleine, woman and awakened girl. She could not have sung as she did, or acted as she did, without a burgeoning from her nature and mind of poetic fruitfulness and swift response to intimations of time and the everyday world of civilised men and women. The art of opera was not enough to give freedom and expression to all her emotional and intellectual needs. She has tried to create first-hand; that is to say, she has sought for realization of her full self and the gifts lavished on her by herself writing poetry, of which I quote this example:

'Und morgen wird die Sonne wieder scheinen' . . .
Wie oft hab' ich das Lied gesungen,
Indes du, siech und krank,
Um Atem hast gerungen
Allein und todesbang . . .
Wir glaubten an den Tag, den einen,
Der uns versprochen und verheissen:
Dass du, zurückgegeben
Dem schönen, so geliebten Leben,
Mit mir am Strande stehst im Sonnengleissen.
Ich neige mein Gesicht in stillem Weinen,
Singe ich jetzt dies Lied:
Dir, der für immer von mir schied,
Wird nie die Sonne wieder scheinen . . .

'And tomorrow the sun will shine again.'
How often have I sung that song
While you, in pain and sickness,
Fought for each breath,
Alone, afraid of death.
Our hopes were fixed upon the day,
That day long promised and vouchsafed to us,
When you, restored to life in all its glorious fullness,
Would stand with me upon the sunlit shore.
I bow my head in silent tears
And sing again that old, remembered song.
For you, now gone from me forever,
The sun will never shine again . . .

A voice from a temporarily vanished habitat. A voice, I hope, to be heard by the ineffable Ginsburg. Lehmann, exiled in California physically, is for me one of the ghosts of Vienna, a shade which mingles with the city's spectral revisitors, at night, after the day is done and the package-tourists have departed. Let me, with Lotte, wallow in nostalgia; we are both old enough to look back, not in anger, but in happy gratitude. Let Lehmann sing for me now, in her own words, suiting my memories to hers, and stirring yet again the exquisite ache at the sense of, and acceptance of, time inexorably passing and taking away:

Ob jetzt an meinen Fenstern die Geranien
In rote Blüten übergeh'n?
Ob wohl im Prater die Kastanien
In tausend weissen Kerzen steh'n?
Wie oft sind wir zu zweit geritten
In frischer, herber Morgenluft
Durch seel'ges Blumenüberschütten,
Durch grüner Bäume würz'gen Duft . . .
Es hingen in den Mähnen uns'rer Pferde
Kastanienblüten, taumelnd, windzerzaust.
Auf spritzte von den Hufen braune Erde,
Wenn galoppierend wir dahingebraust
Durch die Allee, die lange, waldumsäumte . . .
Ach, dass ich wieder von dir träumte,
Du schöne Stadt im Frühlingsblüh'n . . .
Mein Wien!

Are the geraniums now blooming
In scarlet profusion at my windows?
Have the chestnut trees lighted
Their thousand white candles in Prater?
How often have we ridden together
Amid that heavenly galaxy of flowers,
Amid the scented fragrance of green trees,
In the fresh, sharp air of morning!
Wind-scattered, petal on petal,
The chestnut blossom clings to our horses' manes.
The dark earth flies beneath their hooves
As we gallop together like the wind
Along the avenue, the long, tree-bordered avenue . . .
Ah, that I might dream of you again,
Loveliest of cities in the flower'd Spring!
My Vienna!

We are young and the spring morning is young. The sun dapples the leaves of the trees. The open air restaurant in the Stadtpark is animated and, we could think, everlasting. We are unaware of any part of our physical system. We take for granted that the heart is perpetually beating, the lungs clear, our eyes bright and far-seeing. Over there, at a shaded table, sit Arnold Rosé and Buxbaum. We bow to them; but they are aged. We respect them, but nonetheless they are beings apart. We can see a long avenue of years before us; if we for a moment can think ourselves out of the present, this present absorption in ourselves, this marvellous enjoyment of just *ourselves*. Yet behind our backs, so to say, the sand is running out in the hour glass. There is not, in all literature, a more poignant cry from the heart than that of Goethe's Faust: 'Verweile doch, du bist so schön!' Lotte Lehmann's 'altmodisch' poems of sentiment recapture for me a moment in which I was visited by grace, and vouchsafed participation in an experience of the spirit and imagination, removing me, with bitter-sweet brevity, from the illusory delights of self-consciousness and indulgence in actively present mind and emotional responses. In the brown of an autumn afternoon, I went to the Friedhof outside Vienna, the heavenly-named cemetery. There is a small space hedged round by cypress tress, the resting-place of Hugo Wolf, under waving leaves, leaves falling as I stood there, the grave of Anakreon.

Then I returned to the revolving world, and walked back, in the afterglow of the sun, to Vienna. If, in my dying moments, I am able to remember any passage of my writing at all, I pray it will be this one:

'. . . to walk from Grinzing down to Vienna on a September evening, as twilight deepens and the lights of the city begin to twinkle; and to feel the sense of the past, almost to hear the vanishing beauty and song, whispering in the rustle of leaf or wind; and in some hurrying footsteps on the roadside; to feel an awareness to all the hearts that have beaten here, the hopes and the strivings in these old houses, huddled in deserted gardens; the birth and marriage and death; the comings-home at the day's end, the glow of the candlelight and wine and fellowship that surely seemed perennial; the security of life at the crest. And now not only dead but lost to a world which must always be up-and-doing—this, for me, is to live and "go places". Thus has Lotte's poem renewed not only *her* old age but mine: "Ach, dass ich wieder von dir träumte . . ." '

GREEN THOUGHTS IN A GREEN SHADE

To Margaret

Cricket of Vintage

It is pretty certain that if I were young today I wouldn't become devoted to first-class cricket and wish to write about it. The game has usually reflected the national status of economy and social structure. Since round about 1960, cricket, in the organised form in which it is presented to the public, has been changed so much that W. G. Grace would not know it was cricket at all; in fact, it is now not always recognisable by, say, Denis Compton as the game he himself enriched only yesteryear. Cricket has responded, as ever, to the *Zeitgeist*; it has developed a routine standardised efficiency at the expense of the personal touch. It has lost the leisureliness of the aristocratic manner (A. C. MacLaren and Peter May); it has lost humour and county identity (Trueman, Jim Sims and 'Patsy' Hendren). It is offering itself in one-day hit-or-miss scrambles in which winning or losing points or awards is the only appeal to the spectator; for, in such circumstances, style, spaciousness and variety of technique are not free to show themselves; in fact, are discouraged. A slow spin bowler as gifted as Rhodes would seldom get a chance to develop his craft in one-day 'instant' cricket. Imagine any subtly-minded spin bowler dedicated to a species of cricket which limits the number of overs he may bowl in the opponents' innings.

Once upon a time, in a match between South Australia and New South Wales, the patient, conniving leg-spinner 'Clarrie' Grimmett was at his exercises on a hot day. He had got two New South Wales wickets before lunch; then Bradman (at this time one of the New South Wales team) rooted himself at the wicket and blossomed (or blazed) in company with the elegant Alan Kippax. A prolonged and prosperous stand was made by these two master batsmen. But Clarrie persisted with his wiles, tossing up the ball with almost sinful temptation, twisting his fingers over after over, racking his brains. But in vain. So at last his captain, the lamented Victor Richardson, came to him saying: 'Well bowled, Clarrie, but we'll have a change at this end.' Clarrie was aghast. 'What—are you a takin' me orf?' 'Well, Clarrie,' replied Richardson tolerantly, 'you've been bowling since noon.' Clarrie spat on the grass. 'Aw, I got you two wickets this morning, didn't I? And now—if you aren't takin' me orf! Just as I was workin' out my plan.' Working out his plan! No time for such personal indulgences and pride in craft in these speeding 1970s. Three-day cricket matches are naturally alien to the temper and tempo of an age in which men can go to the moon, and come back from the moon, in a shorter time than was needed, not so long ago, to get an England cricket team to Australia and an Australian team to England. 'Instant' cricket, 'instant' everything. The Southern Railway of England has lived to think of trains covering its hallowed rails at 100 miles an hour. But the line is immaterial; or the occupation. The long-timed cricket match, day after day of it, is as dated as the long symphony in music, or the three-volume novel. In 'instant' cricket there is no scope for the great architect batsman, the Leonard Huttons, the C. B. Frys, the Bradmans, who truly symphonised batsmanship, so that we could sit back (untroubled by myopic competitive blind spots) and admire the development, the transitions, a comprehensive display of a master batsman's skill, with the fascination of style that is the man himself holding us throughout the day. Round about 1900–1902 Sussex, playing Lancashire at Brighton, were down on the mat at close of play the second afternoon, which was Friday. (Thursday starts those days.) Only three wickets or so were left for the Lancashire bowlers to take; Sussex needed 150 to save themselves from defeat by an innings. And Ranjitsinhji would be unable to bat again because of an injured left wrist. The Lancashire side looked forward, naturally, to a comfortable

railway journey home on the Sunday to the North. As a fact,
Ranjitsinhji decided on Saturday to bat, one-handed. He
scored 200, frustrating Lancashire's grip on victory, and keeping them in Brighton all day. C. B. Fry was fond of narrating
the details of this marvellous innings of Ranjitsinhji. 'Though it
is well known,' he would emphasise, 'that "Ranji" scored 200
one-handed on a vicious wicket, protecting the other batsmen;
though it is a well-known fact that he achieved this marvellous
innings despite a damaged left wrist; it is not so well known that
he was suffering from an even more serious physical disability—
corns!'

Such cricket, individual and beyond competitive values or
the awards of Horlick and Rothman, was the natural product
of a period and a social climate. Any activity of life is an organism in an environment. MacLaren's batsmanship was as
Edwardian as Elgar's music. In the 1970s, the John Edriches
and Boycotts hint of the computerisation of human skill, and
the practice of it. Nature endows us with equal lavishness of
gifts in all ages, gives us our various skills unstintedly. She
doesn't say: 'I'll bestow special propensities in the 1930s and
withdraw them in 1960.' No, it is the use we put her skills to, a
use too much conditioned by environment pressures. A Victor
Trumper, a Ranjitsinhji, a Compton, each was a sort of cricketer-
artist which our present environment in this country could no
more produce than the 1900s and 1930s could produce a computer or a John Lennon or a dismal, boring Canterbury cricket
Festival. It is not an accident that the freest cricketers, least conditioned by soul-destroying pressures active in sport in Great
Britain today, are not English born or bred. I do not live in the
past; let me see Pollock, Richards, Kanhai, Sobers, Greig,
Lloyd (to name a few) at their best, and I know that cricket is
still capable, given the climate and environment, of producing
a Trumper, a Macartney, a Tom Graveney, a Stanley McCabe.
In England we are obsessed economically and spiritually by
spell-binding 'national devaluation'. Shorter innings in cricket,
individually and collectively. Shorter boundaries. No cricketer
these days can score 2000 runs and take 200 wickets in one and
the same season. George Hirst achieved this dual performance

in the summers of 1904 and 1905; and he was not a lethargic bowler or batsman. When somebody asked him if he thought the dual performance would be equalled by any cricketer in the future, he replied: 'Whoever does it will be tired.' The performance of 2000 runs and 100 wickets, in fact, has been accomplished by W. G. Grace, C. L. Townsend, G. L. Jessop, Rhodes, Tarrant, J. W. Hearne, Woolley, James Langridge, V. W. C. Jupp, L. F. Townsend, E. Davies and Trevor Bailey. Seldom, now, are 1000 runs scored and 100 wickets taken by any one cricketer. Harry Parks of Sussex amazingly amassed 3000 runs and helped himself to 101 wickets in the summer of 1937. I am rather at a loss to account for Trevor Bailey's 100 wickets taken in a season in which he scored 2011 runs, in 1959; because he spent so much time compiling, or secreting, his runs as batsman. One day he stationed himself at the batting crease for several hours engaged in acquiring 50 odd runs. In my report of this somnambulistic innings, I wrote to the following effect: 'Before he had gathered together 20 runs, a newly-married couple could have left Heathrow and arrived in Lisbon, there to enjoy a honeymoon. By the time Bailey had congealed 50, this happily-wedded pair could easily have settled down in a semi-detached house in Surbiton; and by the time his innings had gone to its close they conceivably might have been divorced.' Nonetheless, Bailey was a character, not an adding-machine. He stonewalled passionately, inveterately; and where human passion is in action, there can be no evaporation of dull, anaesthetic air.

The game of cricket had its finest hours when the result, the team-competitive urge, was least important in its appeal to the public. Cricket came to its Golden Ages in the 1890s onward to 1914; then, during the 1930s. Throughout these decades, the crowds at cricket matches were fascinated by Lockwood bowling at Ranjitsinhji, Rhodes bowling at MacLaren, Larwood bowling at Bradman, Macdonald and Gregory bowling at Woolley, O'Reilly bowling at Hammond, Lindwall bowling at Compton, and so on. It was the match *within* the match that held the eyes of lovers of the game in all parts of the game's territory, in different hemispheres. The score-board, and the awards of

points gained by 'results', were secondary appeals to the lovely
batsmanship of Woolley, the grandeur of MacLaren as he dis-
missed a furious missile of a bumping ball from his presence.
Cricket at first-class levels is independent of the game's end,
won or lost. It is the player dominating a six-hour traffic of
sport who really draws the gate-money, day by day. I see now,
in my mind's eye, the run to bowl of Macdonald, the Australian, light of foot, silent as a cat, as he gathered momentum;
then the wheel of his right arm, and the sinuous flexing of his
wrist. If he took 200 wickets for his adopted county of Lancashire (my county, too), I have only the word of 'Wisden' for
it. Do I add up the notes of a Mozart 'Vivace' to evaluate the
music? To look at the score-board while Hobbs was on view, as
master batsman, was as unimaginatively pedantic as it is to
look at the written score while the 'Eroica' Symphony of
Beethoven is being played in your presence. And only those
critics descendant of Beckmesser ever do that.

My notion to the effect that cricket in its rounded first-class
dimension, from Grace to Sobers, has responded to social and
economic changes at large, and to climate, will be supported
by a survey of matches between Yorkshire and Lancashire; or
as I, a Lancastrian, prefer to put it, between Lancashire and
Yorkshire. Before the war of 1914–1918, this historic game of
'The Roses' had opulence of gesture and presence among its
players, as well as dourness and juice of character. Lord Hawke
was the benevolent dictator of the Yorkshire XI; with him was
the Hon. F. S. Jackson. George Hirst was a professional cricketer,
a 'fellow worker', so were David Denton, J. T. Brown, Haigh,
Washington and each of these Yorkshiremen openly exhibited
personal gusto with bat and ball. So was it in the Lancashire XI
of the same epoch, commanded by A. C. MacLaren, all *panache*
and conscious loftiness; he was the Sir Thomas Beecham of
cricket. His colleagues were R. H. Spooner, Beau Brummel of
batsmen, J. T. Tyldesley (I once, in my 'green and yellow'
period, called him the d'Artagnan of batsmen), A. H. Hornby,
son of A. N. Hornby ('O my Hornby and my Barlow long
ago!'), who went into a cricket match like his father, a hunts-
man after the hounds. Also there was Walter Brearley, a roaring

image of humanity, a fast bowler as though in a perpetual gale. All these Lancashire and Yorkshire batsmen, bowlers and fielders reacted to the diversified social and economic climate; there were distinctions of class, of breeding, of nurturing surroundings. The style was most times the man himself. The Lancashire and Yorkshire matches, round about 1904–1914, were tournaments; Canterbury Festivals transported to the North of England.

After 1919, the 'Roses' match began to put *panache* and the gesture of free-willed enjoyable participation behind, as so many vain things. Life in the North country suffered economic depression, following the war supposed fought to end all wars. The 'amateur' influence consequently was dispersed. Today the mere thought of a 'Hon.' or a 'Lord' in a Yorkshire XI is a fantasy. Yet, in place of the old sense of a tourney in Lancashire and Yorkshire matches, a type of character and attitude entered as true to county pressure of nature and economy, as true as anything witnessed in the representative cricket of the Shires in the stratified 1900s. Cricket in Lancashire and Yorkshire in the changing economic set-up after 1919 told us of life and accent evolving in towns and villages, in Bolton, Laisterdyke, Kirkheaton, Westhoughton. The Lancashire and Yorkshire match continued to hold up the mirror. At Bank Holidays, crowds of 30,000 packed the cricket grounds of Old Trafford, Headingley, Bramhall Lane, Park Avenue—and what did these crowds come forth to see? 'Bright cricket'? There was a decade, 1929–1939, when the wicket at Old Trafford was so much a batsman's feather-bed, stuffed with runs, that the Lancashire and Yorkshire match seldom was finished; that is to say, the argument concentrated on a first-innings decision. The brain of Lancashire cricket then was that of Harry Makepeace. 'We've won toss, lads', he would say to his professional colleagues in the Lancashire dressing-room. 'Now, play steady. No fours before lunch.' The cricket correspondent of *The Times*, none other than the scholarly A. C. M. Croome who once played cricket for Gloucestershire as a young man, under the scrutiny of W. G. Grace, came one summer to Old Trafford to watch a Lancashire *v.* Yorkshire match on August Bank Holiday. After lunch, towards 3 o'clock, Lancashire had cunningly contrived to score no more than roughly 100 runs for 1 wicket; the humour of it all was that these highly-skilled Lancashire batsmen, Makepeace, Hallows and Ernest Tyldesley, could have scored runs more quickly had they wished; they 'played steady' against the ancient enemy 'on principle'. Towards 3 o'clock, on this sundrenched August Bank Holiday, Rhodes bowled six consecutive maiden overs; the score-board was static. In the press box (no typewriters) Croome broke silence. 'Why,' he asked, indicating the packed mass of spectators, 'why do they come to watch this sort of cricket on a holiday? Have they all no homes?' 'But why,' I asked him, 'why shouldn't they come?' 'The score-board hasn't moved for a quarter of an hour,' protested Croome, 'the game is moribund.' I told him where he was wrong. 'You take no notice of the score-board when watching Lancashire and Yorkshire. Look at the players. All kinds of personal and feudal animosities are being settled out there. All varieties of North country humour and chicanery are to be witnessed. Look at Rhodes. He is bringing to his bowling the experience of a life time, scheming to keep Makepeace quiet. And Makepeace would not hit a cricket ball recklessly if it were presented to him on a plate decorated with parsley.'

It was likewise in the crowd. At one Lancashire and Yorkshire match, a man sat among the denizens of the county, applauding everything, appreciative of good cricket by Lancashiremen and Yorkshiremen alike. He was looked at curiously by the cloth-capped populace surrounding him. At last, he was addressed by a man clearly from the Lancashire hinterland. 'Tha seems to be enjoying thisel' impartial like,' he said. 'Oh, yes,' replied the impartial spectator enthusiastically, 'splendid cricket. Oh, well hit, sir,—ah, well fielded.' 'Say,' asked the man from Ramsbottom, 'tha's not from these parts, are thi? Tha's not from Lankysheer or Yorkshire?' 'Oh, no,' responded the enthusiast. 'I've come up from Brighton.' 'Oh, hast thi?' said the Lancastrian. 'Then let mi tell thi to keep thy clapper shut. *This* match has got nowt to do with *thee*.'

The crowds, like the players, were dedicated to the match, brought up from infancy to it, bred in the air of friendly rivalry which enriched the two counties. The cricketers were household gods; the cricketers of Lancashire and Yorkshire regarded the game as a vocation. Emmott Robinson and Wilfred Rhodes were Yorkshire cricket in apotheosis; each lived for Yorkshire cricket, on the field and off. At Lords, on a Saturday in the mid-1920s, Yorkshire batted from noon to close of play, scoring some 350 runs. On Sunday morning a violent thunderstorm, with heavy rain, was followed by an afternoon of hot sunshine. I went walking in Hyde Park, and I met Emmott and Rhodes. 'Lovely afternoon,' I said, as a greeting to the great men. 'Aye,' snapped Emmott, 'and a "sticky" wicket wa-astin' at Lord's!'

Always must I tell the identifying true story of Emmott, whenever I am making a pen-picture for the delectation of Yorkshire posterity. Following a wet morning at Leeds, with burning sun at two o'clock, Emmott and Rhodes went forth on the field of Headingley to inspect the wicket. I was allowed to go with them. Rhodes pressed the turf with a forefinger. 'Emmott,' he announced, 'it'll be "sticky" at four o'clock.' And Emmott bent down and, with thumb and forefinger, fondled the moist but drying turf. 'No, Wilfred,' he said, '*half-past*.' Dedication, shrewdness, caution, extended to godlike humour. These were 'county' characters, from mill and factory or pit, having horse sense and no more education than was needed in their condition of life. I have for years believed that a man should be thoroughly educated, or not at all. The middle way, 'O' levels and all that, produces anonymous competent mediocrity, enslaved to technology and efficiency. The salt of the county nurture is eliminated. In another Lancashire and Yorkshire match, at Old Trafford, burly Dick Tyldesley made, apparently, a swift catch at short-leg, low to the ground; but immediately he let the umpire and the interested batsman know that the ball had touched the ground, even as his right hand grasped it. In my report of the match I congratulated him on this act of sportsmanship. Next day, I congratulated him personally, by word of mouth. 'Thank you, Maister Cardus,' he replied, 'Westhoughton Sunday School, tha knows.' In this grand remark was contained a summary of Lancashire social

background, of humble domestic ethical instruction. The remark sets the Lancastrian imagination at work, conjuring up
scenes, cobbled streets, Sunday afternoon, the lads and lassies
in their 'Sunday best' clothes. 'Westhoughton Sunday School,
tha knows.' He couldn't have said it, thought of it, in these days,
with a half-education burdening and drying up the nature
given to him bountifully, with a chuckle of delight, by God.

From 1919 to 1939, I was present at all Lancashire *v.* Yorkshire matches, writing some 1500 words about each day's play
—even in wet weather. An August Bank Holiday in Manchester
was gloomy and wet from dawn; no cricket, of course, at Old
Trafford. I did not stir out of my home, until I went to the
Manchester Guardian office as usual at 7 p.m. or thereabouts. The
chief sub-editor, Attenborough, welcomed me smilingly.
'Thank God,' he said, 'there's been a blank day at Old Trafford
—I'm crushed tonight for space.' But I gave him a column,
1200 words, describing what *might* have happened at Old
Trafford that day if the weather had honoured a Lancashire *v.*
Yorkshire match, and what often *had* happened on a day in the
sun. The panorama of these wonderful games, year after year
in my lifetime since boyhood, still moves in my mind photo-
graphically. I can't recall what occurred last year at Old Trafford, or at Leeds, between Lancashire and Yorkshire, but I can
still see, screened on my memory's retina, George Hirst in the
early 1900s. He was given out l.b.w. to an appeal from Walter
Brearley, and everybody adjacent, excepting the umpire, heard
Hirst's bat make contact with the ball before it struck his pads.
Hirst, always with a heart as big as a broadacre, left the wicket
unhesitatingly. But MacLaren chastised Brearley: 'You bloody
fool, Walter; we'll have to pay for this.' Next day when the
second Lancashire innings began, George Hirst rolled up the
sleeve of the Yorkshire ham of his left arm, then bowled Lancashire out for 49, taking 9 wickets. Hirst was one of the most
accomplished cricketers of the game's history; a strong sturdy
batsman, a fastish left-arm inswing bowler, and quick and im-
penetrable at mid-off. Best of all, he was the full Yorkshireman,
as warm-hearted as, in the right circumstances, a stern opponent. At the close of his career as first-class cricketer, he coached

boys at Eton to play cricket. The Headmaster of Eton, then the Reverend Cyril Alington, told me that he himself conducted the correspondence arranging Hirst's appointment. Hirst accepted in some such language as this: 'I am deeply privileged to accept your offer to serve Eton College as cricket coach, and will do my best and be honoured.' Not a word about 'terms', remuneration, salary, wages! Today the 'pro' would be pretty certain to make some stipulation regarding commission on sales of bats, balls, etc. Hirst, naturally as a man born at Kirkheaton, had the humour which can compromise one's moral responsibility. His highest score, as Yorkshire batsman, was 341, against Leicestershire in 1905. It was subsequently stated by watchers of the match that before scoring a run he was l.b.w. Years after the event, in his retirement, I asked him: 'Were you out?' His reply remains a joy to remember and retell. 'It's not for me to question the published records in *Wisden's Cricketers Almanack*.'

At the extreme of Hirst, as cricketer and Yorkshireman, stood Wilfred Rhodes; the two of them together made the assemblable bulk of the county's human nature and character, richness, geniality, shrewdness and an understanding of what pays and what does not pay. Every schoolboy knows, or used to know, of the achievements of Rhodes with bat and ball; a great slow left arm bowler from young manhood to middle age. To begin with, a No. 11 batsman, in last for England, who took part in a record tenth-wicket stand against Australia at Sydney, 130 runs with R. E. Foster, in December 1903; then, in company of the master Jack Hobbs, he held his own as opening batsman scoring 323 with Hobbs, for England against Australia at Melbourne, February 1912, another record. What other cricketer has, with bat, risen to this eminence from the lowliest of positions in a team's batting order? No fewer than twenty-three times Rhodes, in one and the same season, scored 1000 runs and had 100 wickets. Thrice in his career he took 200 wickets in a season. Your Sobers pants and toils after Rhodes in vain for all-round cricket skill; and nobody has equalled Rhodes in understanding of every fine shade of the game. All the tricks of the trade were in his keeping. I make no apology for quoting here a description I wrote of his bowling half a century ago:

'He overthrew the most celebrated batsmen, by subtlety of flight. Flight—the curving line, now higher, now lower, tempting, inimical; every ball like every other ball, yet somehow unlike. Each over in collusion with the rest, part of a plot. Every ball a decoy, a spy sent out to get the lie of the land. Some balls simple, some complex, some easy, some difficult. And one of them—ah, which?—the master ball.'

At the age of ninety, now sightless, I met him at Lord's. He remembered my voice. 'Ah, Ah'm glad to meet you, P'raps you can settle somethin' that's been worryin' me. Were you at that Oval Test when George Hirst and me got the runs 'genst Australia? . . .' 'Of course I wasn't,' I replied, 'I was still at school.' He looked disappointed. 'You see, Ah've been worryin' —Ah pushed a ball from Hughie Trumble, when we only wanted a few to win. And Ah can't remember whether it went for two or for four.' After more than sixty years, he couldn't remember whether the stroke had been worth, to him and England, two or four. As I say, dedication. Once on a time, all Yorkshire children were born that way. At a packed Lancashire and Yorkshire match at Sheffield, a girl fainted because of heat and congestion. The ambulance attendants sprinkled water in her face and she recovered consciousness, blinked her eyes, then asked anxiously: 'Is Sutcliffe out?'

Roy Kilner, a Yorkshire cricketer who died too soon, was, like Hirst, Haigh and David Denton, representative of the softer side of his county's nature, though, of course, not to be 'put upon'; he was Yorkshire with a twinkle. 'In Yorksheer and Lanky matches,' he affirmed to me, 'there's best be no umpires and fair cheatin' all round.' He bowled slow left-arm spin, but he often upset the purists of his day by bowling, on hard pitches, from over the wicket. No classical left-arm spinner of Yorkshire from Peel, Rhodes to Verity, spun the ball from over the wicket. Thereby hangs a gorgeous tale. After poor Roy's funeral, done in high Yorkshire fashion, relations and friends gathered in the parlour, talking of him, loving him, telling gay stories of him. Wilfred Rhodes spoke little, until the moment of his departure for home. 'Aye,' he said, 'we'll miss him, we'll miss him. He used to bowl over wicket for hours, then George Macauley would get 'em all out for nowt in last innin's with his off-spinners!' I would spoil the humour of this remark if I were to give the technical clue; cricketers will see the rich point of it.

Freddie Trueman contributed his pages to Yorkshire history of character, though sometimes he consciously exploited his 'foon'. Rhodes, Emmott, Macaulay and the rest were blissfully unaware of the humour they were spreading about them. So with the Yorkshire crowds, once on a time. In the late summer of 1920, an England team was about to be chosen by the M.C.C. to go to Australia. At Sheffield, on an afternoon of dull cricket —that is to say, the other side would not get out—two Yorkshire spectators relieved themselves of the monotony caused by two obstinate Middlesex batsmen by themselves picking this England XI for Australia. 'Now, 'Arry,' said one, 'we'll want two good op'nin' batters, an' we can't do better than Percy Holmes and 'Erbert Sutcliffe.' 'Aye, Ernest, an' first wicket down batter wants to be good at both games, defendin' an' hittin' ball. And we needn't look farther than Oldroyd.' Solemnly and judiciously, these two Yorkshiremen selected the entire Yorkshire team to represent England in Australia. I could not help overhearing their conversation which was too much for me. So I interrupted. 'Sorry,' I said, 'but you've left out of your England XI Jack Hobbs.' Consternation. 'By gum, 'Arry, so we 'ave. We've been and gone and left Jack Hobbs out.' Harry scratched his head, and admitted, 'Aye, we 'ave.' Then he added: 'But 'ow can we get 'im in?'

As a Lancastrian, I pray that the juice of Yorkshire blood-stock is for ever preserved. And it is my hope that only thorough-bred Yorkshiremen are for ever allowed to wear the cap adorned by the White Rose. I pray and hope the same for Lancashire cricket. I am as anti-apartheid as the next demon-strator or demonstration; nonetheless, I prefer that Yorkshire and Lancashire cricketers should be home-grown, of the soil. As a boy I was enchanted by the dusky legerdemain of Ran-jitsinhji's batting for Sussex; but I didn't like to see him playing for England. As a fact, I, like most Yorkshire and Lancashire folk, thought that the strongest England cricket team was the one including as many Yorkshire and Lancashire players as well could be gathered together—as happened at Manchester in 1905, where and when the England XI *v.* Australia, contained no fewer than seven Lancashire and Yorkshire men: MacLaren, J. T. Tyldesley, F. S. Jackson, R. H. Spooner, G. H. Hirst, W. Rhodes and W. Brearley. I admit that such cosmopolitans as MacLaren, the Hon. F. S. Jackson and R. H. Spooner could have served the then elegant setting of Lord's more fittingly than Sheffield or Old Trafford. It was the lads out of village pits and factory who created the Yorkshire and Lancashire cricket tradition. 'What about Lord Hawke?' I asked Emmott Robinson, as we discussed who and what is real Yorkshire. ' 'E weren't a Yorkshireman to begin with,' snapped Emmott. As Yorkshire as Ilkley Moor was Arthur Wood. He kept wicket. One day, at Fenners, Yorkshire were playing Cambridge University. Macauley clean bowled an undergraduate and, miraculously, the bails were not disturbed. Outraged, the Yorkshire team, in its entirety, inspected the three stumps and the static bails. Arthur Wood blew at them with all his breath. But the umpires waved the Yorkshiremen back to their places in the field. The lucky young undergraduate, marvellously not out, was preparing to receive the next ball from Macauley, when Arthur Wood from behind the stumps addressed him: 'Excuse me, sir, but has ever tried walkin' on water?'—the word 'water' pronounced to rhyme with 'martyr'. Not long ago, the Prime Minister of England, Harold Wilson (Yorkshireman to the bone) spoke at a dinner given to the Australian team in the House of Commons. He was rightly fulsome in his praise of Yorkshire cricket, too fulsome in the opinion of a Lancastrian in the company, who cried out: 'But Mr. Prime Minister, what about Lancashire?' 'I am not interested in the Minor counties,' was the natural and friendly retort of Mr. Wilson. At the same dinner, Harold Wilson informed the Australian cricketers that he had recently described, in a public statement, Freddie Trueman as the greatest living Yorkshireman—'a statement', added Mr. Wilson, 'which, in half an hour, brought me an irate telegram from J. B. Priestley.'

O my Makepeace and my Sutcliffe, long ago!

* * * * *

I am vastly amused to hear modern cricketers maintaining that they play the game more 'scientifically' than it was played decades ago. The 'scientific' bowlers rub the new ball on their buttocks, rendering flannels apparently blood-stained; and down the leg-side they swing the missile, 'using the seam'. In the Rhodes-Hirst-Barnes epoch, the same ball had to be bowled throughout the longest of a team's innings; these masters needed to employ brains, not depend on tools. In the 1900s, Hirst sent down the pitch a new ball with so acute an inswing that, as C. B. Fry described it, it came to the batsman like a fierce throw-in from cover-point. Hirst set a three-man leg-field, close to the wicket. There is nothing new under the sun. Against this attack, while the new ball retained power to swerve, R. H. Spooner flicked heavenly strokes through the encircling leg-side fieldsmen. In his old age, a match was played to celebrate the eightieth birthday of S. F. Barnes, greatest of all bowlers of any time. It was arranged that he should bowl the first ball of this match, sort of ceremoniously. Asked, before the event, how he would bowl this inaugural over, he said: 'Well, at my time of life, and out of practice, I can't spin 'em, so I suppose I'll have to fall back on "seamers".' Any healthy brainless youth can hold a cricket ball with the seam in a certain position, and obtain a 'swerve', one way or the other. This method of bowling is as mechanical, as predictable, as unimaginative, as boring, as the 'serial' set-up of the latest 'modern' composer.

If I could retain on the screen of my memory a film or graphic depiction (in colour, if you like) of an ideal England cricket team, which names and images would I wish to have indefinitely preserved? No doubt of my first choice (I am, of course, selecting my favourite cricketers from those I have actually seen): Jack Hobbs, the Master, in all the varying material circumstances of his career, extending nearly thirty years. When he began to hint of his talent as batsman, the attack was Victorian in its observance of classic first principles to good length pitched on the wicket, or just outside the off-stump, very fast, or medium pace, or slow spin on ground hard and bouncing in dry weather, but vicious after rain and sun; no covering of pitches then. As a fact, Hobbs learned the game in the presence of W. G. Grace who, if not instructing him and all others personally, did so by indirect influence. For 'W.G.' more or less established the Law, the Tablets of cricket throughout the nineteenth century. In the mid-1900s, swerve of flight was developed by bowlers when a new ball could be demanded after the batting side had scored 200. In 1907, the craft of 'googly' was advanced in skill and obliquity by B. J. T. Bosanquet, Vogler, Aubrey Faulkner, Hordern. All these new bowling skills were mastered by Hobbs, on matting wickets in South Africa, on spinning sun-and-rain-bedevilled turf in England and Australia. He was seldom seen to perform a hurried stroke. I never saw him guilty of an ugly, ungrammatical stroke. He would lose his wicket, being human, by error of judgment, producing the right stroke for the wrong ball. Other batsmen abide our question; he is free. My next choice for my dream of an England XI, to open an innings with the Master, is George Gunn. (Let me here emphasise that I am picking a team *not* primarily to win a match, but to give me the satisfaction of looking at personal art and artifice; nonetheless, I fancy that my XI, after I have shaped it, would be very hard to cope with.) George Gunn was the wittiest, the most unpredictable of batsmen, brilliant, casual, supremely independent by turn. Whenever he set his mind to play seriously, he could stand comparison with the Master himself. 'The trouble with most batsmen,' he told me, in his old age, 'is that they worry too much about the state of the pitch, prodding it and so encouraging the bowler. What's more, there's another trouble with batsmen, always has been, ever since I played, and I played with Doctor Grace. They take too much notice of the bowling.'

My first wicket down batsman is, of course, Hammond, at his best mingling power of back foot and sinuous wrist. I need say no more of him, except to remind one and all that he was a slip fieldsman beyond compare, and as dangerous bowling a new ball as most. Next, at No. 4, I must have in my great company Denis Compton, masterly without pomposity, sometimes without maturity, constantly renewing himself, so that he could, at one and the same time, show us batsmanship or rare technical range, rendered almost boyish by impulse. In the mastery of

Hobbs something of autumnal brown appeared; in the mastery of Compton the green leaf wonderfully revealed itself again and again.

Now I come to a quandary in my selection. The Captain. I fall for A. C. MacLaren, with apologies to the shades of P. F. Warner and D. R. Jardine. MacLaren was the most lordly of them all, a *grand seigneur* at the wicket, the bowler and the fieldsmen his menials. In our modern times we have seen only one cricketer faintly reminiscent of MacLaren and he was Ted Dexter. But Dexter, a product of a period shorn of aristocratic *panache* was, compared to MacLaren in demeanour and cricket breeding, a sort of gentleman's gentleman. His show of command and hauteur seemed to be obtained second-hand, so to say; he could be brilliant and admirable for a period, but not often over a long innings. Blue blood, yes; also a *bar sinister*. Frank Woolley next, please. Imagine Woolley coming in to bat No. 6; all grace, hiding punitive strength. I pick him as an all-rounder who could score 2000 runs and take 100 wickets in one and the same season. Wilfred Rhodes, also as acquisitive with bat as with ball, comes into my XI free-willed, so to say; so do Godfrey Evans, wicket-keeper of ubiquitous movement and opportunism, and Larwood, Tate and S. F. Barnes, an attack fit to bowl in Parnassus against Trumper, Ranjitsinhji, Grace and Stanley McCabe. The missing link in the attack is leg-spin. I am reminded, as I note this lack, of the retort of Barnes, when I told him that he had been compared as a bowler, to his disadvantage, with O'Reilly, the Australian. 'O'Reilly had all the Barnes repertory, *plus* the "googly",' maintained an authority. 'True,' admitted Barnes, 'I did not bowl the googly. I never needed it.'

Now, as I contemplate on paper my England XI of Incomparables, I am ashamed that I have cast out glories of my youth, my Lancastrians, Spooner and Tyldesley, whose very shoes I would have worshipped because they trod on the green grass of Old Trafford. And where are Tom Richardson, C. B. Fry, Blythe, Hedley Verity and the shining lights in our own time— Trueman, Statham, Peter May, Colin Cowdrey and Leonard Hutton? I am obliged to echo the Yorkshireman in the crowd at Sheffield: 'But 'ow could we get 'em in?' How indeed?

I have mentioned Hedley Verity who, like Colin Blythe, also a beautiful left-arm bowler, died fighting for his country, aged thirty-eight, as young as Blythe. He was in conversation, as on the field in action, a quiet Yorkshireman, seldom argumentative. His movements were always unobtrusive, almost studious. On board ship to Australia, he would sit alone in a deckchair reading Lawrence's *Seven Pillars of Wisdom*. In 1934, at Lord's against Australia, he wrecked Australia's innings twice, taking 15 wickets for 104, reducing Bradman himself to a desperate agitation of footwork astonishing to see. I went into the pavilion to congratulate Verity; and he received my handshake by saying: 'I did my best. It's an honour to play for England.' I find this remark difficult to put across nowadays; it sounds so much like J. M. Barrie at his worst, or like Mr. Chips, if it comes to that. Spoken by Verity, the saying was lovable, natural and true.

He was aptly named, though Emmott Robinson once asked: 'Where did he get Hedley from?' He was not without humour, the humour of character, not to be expressed by anything so crude as a loud laugh. He twinkled; when he ran to bowl his steps were light, cat-like, without material weight to be moved. From his fingers spun a ball of secretive guile, whipping away on a responsive turf, and lifting spitefully at an acute angle. There was comedy (in the eyes and mind of the watcher) to note the contrast of Verity's quite gentlemanly mien as he bowled, and the horrid spitting venom of his bowling. He could turn satire on himself.

On a certain Test match occasion *v.* South Africa, his bowling was severely punished by Cameron, South Africa's superb batsman-wicket-keeper. After this match I journeyed to London with Verity, who was due to play there also against South Africa. Verity, a theorist, propounded to me a plan whereby he would surely ensnare Cameron. 'He could hit across my line of flight on a slow paced wicket; but at Lord's, where it is faster, I'll be able to bounce the ball, and Cameron will hit across at the rise, and I'll have him caught at back square-leg.' But at Lord's Cameron hit Verity's bowling not once but several times into the Mound Stand; and at close of play Verity said to me, with delightful rueful relish of what he was saying: 'It's Cameron who's been doing the bouncing today.'

Though Yorkshire as much in the bone as the rest, Rhodes or Robinson, Verity did not deafen the umpire whenever he appealed for l.b.w. or catch at the wicket decision. He would turn on his heel and put his question to the umpire *sotto voce*, with his fingers apologetically in front of his mouth. Yet if he could be called a 'classical' slow left-arm spinner because of the balance and style of his action, he did not follow in the truly classical line of Peel and Rhodes. Verity's pace was medium rather than slow, no hovering in its flight as the flight of Rhodes and Peel did, like some bird of ill-omen and temptation. It was Verity's direction down to the pitch from his tall height that made it difficult for batsmen to cope with his spin and lift on a 'sticky' wicket. In the year of Verity's first appearance for Yorkshire, I stood behind the bowler's arm at Leeds one day, studying Verity's methods. Maurice Leyland (Yorkshire *in excelsis*) came to me and, after watching with me for a while, asked: 'Well, and what dost think of our new *fast* bowler?' The great Rhodes himself visited Lord's, especially to take the measure of Verity; he was now a coach at Harrow. He scrutinised Verity closely, as Verity bowled on a flawless batsman's pitch. 'Aye,' muttered Wilfred, 'he's a good 'un, aye, he's a good 'un. And he can bowl one ball as I never could.' In astonishment we asked him, 'Good Lord, Wilfred, can he? Which ball is it?' 'The one which batsmen can tickle round to leg for a single. . . .'

For all his air of the perpetual student, Verity belonged to the lighter side of Yorkshire cricket, leavening the dour lump according to nature's beneficent law of compensation. He was an artist at bottom; but no doubt he kept to himself, and did not share the knowledge with Rhodes and Robinson, the fact that he loved to bowl just for the sake of bowling. A Yorkshire victory might be a consequence of his fine art, but for him the result of a match was a secondary consideration. On a perfect turf he once, I remember, bowled for hours, and took not a single wicket. At the end of the hot day I spoke to him, deploring his lack of success. 'Impossible to turn the ball on that feather-bed of a wicket,' I said. With quiet satisfaction he replied: 'But I was spinning it at my end,' meaning that his fingers had all the time been exquisitely in play, like Kreisler's. Another case of unheard melodies.

He was a great friend of William or 'Bill' Bowes, Yorkshire fast bowler in Verity's period. These two grand Yorkshiremen and cricketers were Jonathan and David in the game's encircling friendliness. I think that Bowes worshipped Verity as a schoolboy worships an unapproachable hero. But Bowes has an openness of character, an embracing Yorkshire confidence in you, not uninhibitedly expressed by Verity. At Brisbane in the press box in 1946, Bowes was for the first time working as a reporter. A terrible thunderstorm ended play for the afternoon towards five o'clock, conveniently allowing the press time in which to write and send cables to England. At the desk behind me, Bowes was in the throes of parturition. He leaned over the desk nervously and said: 'Do you mind looking at my copy? I'm a new boy at this job.' I took his report and read: 'The sky darkened, the lightning forked to earth, and heaven's artillery thundered, and soon conditions became unfit for further play . . .' 'Very good, Bill.' I said to him, reassuringly, 'Very good.' 'Aye,' he said, taking back his copy gingerly, 'aye, it begins all right—but then it goes away to nothin'.' Lovable, honest as the day. At Leeds, Bowes in the day's last hour removed three Australian wickets out of England's path for next to nothing. Next morning, Bradman drove straight and powerfully, without effort, the first two balls in Bowes's first over for fours. 'I never bowled two better balls,' maintains Bowes, 'the seam was still there, and the shine. Never bowled two better balls. So I knew Bradman *had* me—what's more, I knew he had me *for the day*.' He was right in this assumption. Bradman scored a triple century. I relate Bowes's engaging confession: 'I knew he had me for the day,' to convey as strongly as I can, by pen on paper, the precious stuff he is made of; and I relate it in hope that the shade of Hedley Verity may hear of it, and spiritually revisit his Yorkshire terrestrial soil, and join in with Bill Bowes's laughter of good companionship.

C. B. Fry

The most remarkably gifted man ever to give to cricket many years of his life—and he was eighty-four when he died in 1956—was Charles Burgess Fry. As batsman he amassed some 30,000 runs, averaging fifty an innings. Bradman equalled Fry's achievement of 1901—six hundreds in six consecutive innings—and, no doubt, Sobers could perform the same extraordinary feat were he to give his mind to it. But neither Bradman nor Sobers has had the versatility of skill and brain to send translations of the English Hymnal to *The Times*, as Fry did, and to appear as a delegate at the Assembly of the League of Nations in Geneva, deputising for Ranjitsinhji, who represented India; what is more, Fry at this Assembly composed a speech which when delivered contributed to Mussolini's removal from Corfu. Other activities of Fry, taken in his stride, were to win first-class Honours in Classical Moderations at Wadham; to put himself forward as a Liberal candidate in a parliamentary election for Brighton and to poll—in Brighton, mark you—20,000 votes; to receive an invitation to take the kingdom of Albania; to direct a training-ship for the Royal Navy (and to produce on it a concert performance of *Parsifal*); to edit a monthly magazine; to hold for years the world's long-jump record; to play soccer for England against Ireland; and, of course, to play cricket for England.

One morning, in his seventieth year, he came into his club and joined Denzil Batchelor and me at the bar. 'Ah, Denzil,' he said, 'I'm feeling like Alexander. I've done most things. I

sigh for a new world to conquer. I think I'll go into the Turf.'
Batchelor replied, with rapid wit: 'In what capacity, Charles?
As owner, trainer, jockey or horse?'

He came from the late-Victorian social climate in which
countless Englishmen, fathers of families, seemed able to get by
economically on little or nothing a year, considered as fixed
earned income. In this period, players of first-class cricket in
England were 'amateur' or 'professional', terms not referring to
different levels of skill among the performers, but marking a
class distinction. The amateur gave his summers to county
cricket, receiving no emoluments save his travelling expenses.
In the Kent XI, for example, there were usually eight amateurs,
the professionals (Blythe, Huish and Fairservice) getting places
by entrance, so to say, to the servants' quarters. Fry, indeed,
was one of the last of a breed, amateur in the strictest philosophical meaning of the word, not bound by or subject to the
servitude of professional skill, but sometimes free of it because
skill had come his way as a sort of inspired dilettantism. Yet
here is the Fry paradox; when Fry devoted himself to batsmanship he disciplined himself with an almost austere regard for
first principles of technique. He wrote a book on batsmanship
of Aristotelean logic and ethical responsibility. He was the first
student of cricket to canonise the injunctions: 'Play back or
drive.' 'Watch the ball and direct the stroke at the ball itself,
not at a point in space where you hope the ball will presently
be.' This was the 'revolutionary' doctrine which, in time, produced Bradman. The classic lunge forward, extending the
batsman to a point where stretching allowed little freedom of
reverse action, and where the position of the ball could only
be guessed at, fell into obsolescence by the truly great batsmen.

Fry was so much the student, or thinker, of batsmanship that
frequently he appeared less interested in the runs he was scoring
than in the problems of bowling as presented to his intellect, as
though in the abstract. Only by staying at the crease a considerable time could he arrive at the mental detachment necessary
for scrutiny as objectively perceived as this; his centuries *accrued*
as a by-product. No thought of personally achieved records or
aggrandisement of runs ever occurred to him. He was absorbed

in the *rationale* of cricket, absorbed in the fundamentals. Frank Woolley, incomparably lovely left-handed Kent batsman of all time, relates how once he bowled at Fry on a nasty 'turning' pitch (let it be remembered that Woolley was also a masterful left-arm slow spinner). 'I beat Mr. Fry several times without bowling him. Then, to my astonishment, he explained to me why I was not getting him out. He demonstrated that I was not pitching the ball on the right spot, and that it was bounding *over* the stumps in consequence.' Fry was solving Woolley's problems for him.

He was, of course, seen day by day in conjunction with K. S. Ranjitsinhji, scoring runs for Sussex plenteously as the sun mounted the June sky to noon and went down to evening. 'There were no eyes for me,' Fry confessed, 'I played in "Ranji's" shadow.' At one end of the wicket Ranjitsinhji changed batsmanship into an act of legerdemain from the Orient; Fry was rationally of the Occident, scoring by the book of arithmetic. But his driving was majestic. 'They maintained that I had only one stroke,' he said to me, 'maybe—but it went to ten different parts of the field.' We can best estimate the skill of Fry by recording that against the Yorkshire XI of the 1900s, the most dangerous of all for destructive bowling manipulated by Hirst, Rhodes, Haigh, Wainwright and F. S. Jackson; against this attack Fry scored nearly 2500 runs in all, average 70. In 1903, he scored 234 against Yorkshire at Bradford; next summer, against Yorkshire, he scored 177 at Sheffield and 229 at Brighton in successive innings. It is hard to convey in words today the national astonishment felt in the 1900s by cricketers as Fry went his predetermined processional way—3147 runs in 1901, average 78; in 1903, 2683 runs, average 81. When I was a schoolboy I did not think of Fry as an ordinary man. On the field of play he was an animate Phidias, a living sculpture of upright masculine handsomeness, all of him alert, elastic, with a hint of a Sir Willoughby Patterne *hauteur*. As he fielded on the boundary at third-man, waiting for the bowler to get to work, he would make movement of his toes indicating an incipient waltz. As he went in chase of a ball, his long strides, loose and easy, kept the indignity of hurry at bay. His aquiline face was brown, and the eyes ever keen and bright. He was an artist in attitudes, vain and delighted in his own poised movements of self-mastery. After making an on-drive, he would stand, bat aloft, on an unseen yet obviously present pedestal, contemplating the direction and grandeur of the stroke. The cricket field has seen no sight more Grecian than the sight presented by Charles Burgess Fry. Irony of crude material events mocked him in 1902, mocked Prince Ranjitsinhji as wickedly. At Lord's that year, England played Australia. I ran out of school to see the score in a newspaper; no radio then. I, and England all over, stood shocked at the tidings:

C. B. Fry c Hill b Hopkins 0
K. S. Ranjitsinhji   b   Hopkins 0

The demi-gods out for nothing! What was the more unbelievable, the demi-gods were exposed as mortal and perishable by an Australian named Hopkins. Just before his life's end Fry sat one day in his club, remembering an innings he played at Lord's, round about 1900, for Sussex against Middlesex. 'At close of play,' he said, 'I had scored 80 or thereabouts, and next morning Albert Trott clean bowled me first over with an off-break.' Whereat Fry got up from his chair and went through the motions of a batsman coping with an off-break. And, as he went through these motions, unseen bat in his grip, he said: 'Yes, he clean bowled me with an off-break. I can't think what I was doing; can't think what I was doing.' Half a century after the event, his mind was still vexed and baffled. He was not only the Sir Willoughby Patterne of cricket; something of Hamlet was mixed in his elements. A great Englishman, measured by any standards of occupation, art and civilisation.

Arthur Mailey

The most fascinating cricketer I have known was the Australian Arthur Mailey, an artist in every part of his nature. On the field of play, he bowled leg-spin, with the 'googly'. A man of his gift for fantasy could never have contented himself with 'seaming' a new ball. Mailey would tell me how much he revelled in the 'feel' of a ball spinning from his fingers. 'I'd rather spin and see the ball hit for four than bowl a batsman out by a straight one.' Such a view or attitude was not exactly attuned to the main idea (the only idea nowadays) obsessing a cricketer: the lust for victory, the fear of defeat. Yet Mailey could win a match devastatingly, spinning the greatest batsmen to immobile helplessness. Once he bowled Gloucestershire out single-fingered, or rather, with three fingers and a thumb. He took all ten wickets in a Gloucestershire innings for 66. Then, later, when he wrote his autobiography, he called the book *10 for 66, and All That*.

His life as a boy was not unlike my own, born in a semi-slum, the so-called Surry 'hills', a Sydney excretion, eighty years ago. He was 'dragged up', and worked as a labourer, a plumber's mate, at any casual job. All the time he educated himself, learned not only the most difficult sort of bowling; also he cultivated a talent to paint pictures and draw cartoons. He became, at the height of his career as cricketer, a well-liked cartoonist in Sydney newspapers. He sketched in the manner of the 1890s, broad and unsubtle, yet humorous. He painted landscape canvases, with trees and skies recognisably green, brown or blue. In London, he had a private exhibition of his paintings. Queen Mary did him the honour of inspecting these landscapes. She was graciously approving, on the whole; but she paused in front of one canvas, saying: 'I don't think, Mr. Mailey, you have painted the sun quite convincingly in this picture.' 'Perhaps not, Your Majesty,' replied Arthur, 'you see, Your Majesty, in this country I have to paint the sun from memory.'

'If ever I bowl a maiden over,' he assured me, 'it's not my fault, but the batsman's.' He enjoyed himself; he explored himself; he was whimsical. One Saturday in Sydney I saw him on the ferry boat going to Neutral Bay, a mile or two's journey—it couldn't be called a voyage. We chatted and parted at our suburban destination. A few days later, I read in a newspaper that he had arrived in London—in wartime. Not a word had he spoken, as we journeyed that Saturday afternoon to Neutral Bay, of his flight to London. I would run into him at Lord's, not during a tour of an Australian team here, run into him and cry out in surprise, 'Good Lord, Arthur, what are you doing in London? When did you come?' 'Oh,' he would say, 'I've just dropped in from Hong Kong—via Neutral Bay.' He was slender of physical build, well-shouldered; his face good-looking, with a touch of aboriginal, was wrinkled with incipient fun. He never laughed loudly; he smiled, as the play of his whimsical mind tickled his nerve of risibility. He was one of the New South Wales bowlers pitted against Victoria at Melbourne, in the Australian summer of 1926–1927, in the match in which Victoria amassed 1107 runs in a single innings. Mailey contrived to take 4 wickets for round about 350 runs; but, he maintained to his life's end, the scorer's analysis on the occasion did him less than justice, because three catches were missed off his bowling—'two by a man in the pavilion, wearing a bowler hat.'

He tossed up his spin to the batsman slow and alluringly; never have I seen on a cricket field such undisguised temptation as was presented to the batsman by Mailey's bowling. It was almost immoral. He once clean bowled the incomparable Hobbs with a slow full toss, also at Melbourne, after the Master and Herbert Sutcliffe had scored 283 together, undefeated, on the third day of the second Test match of the 1924–1925 rubber.

First ball next day Hobbs missed Mailey's full 'floater'. Mailey needed to double-up his body to express the humour of it. If a catch was dropped from his bowling, he seldom complained; he would go to the unhappy fieldsman and say: 'I'm expecting to take a wicket any day now.' No bowler has spun a ball with more than Mailey's twist, fingers and right forearm and leverage. He lacked the accuracy of, say, Grimmett, another Australian leg-spinner; but Mailey bowled his spin with the lavishness of a millionaire. Grimmett bowled it like a miser—as Ray Robinson, Australia's wittiest cricket writer, once put it, or suggested the simile, to me.

At the end of March 1948, I was one of the company of Bradman's Australian team sailing by Orient line to England, Bradman's last summer in England as cricketer. His team was indeed powerful, for in it were two great fast bowlers, Lindwall and Miller, with Johnston in support. The batsmen collaborating with Bradman included Morris, Barnes, Hassett, Harvey, Brown, Miller and Loxton. During the voyage, one evening after dinner, Bradman sat talking to a number of his players. One of them said, in an excess of pride that he was one of the chosen few, 'You've got a great side for this trip, Don. I doubt if Victor Trumper could have got a place in it.' The Don contemplated this remark for a few seconds. 'I don't agree,' he said quietly, 'no, I don't agree. Victor could have got it all right.' 'But,' persisted the proud one, 'who could you drop out of this present team for Trumper?' Like a flash Bradman replied, '*You*—to begin with.' Memorable and ruthless.

Arthur Mailey had now, of course, retired from active service on the field, but he was with us on the way to England in that spring of 1948. We sat at the same dining-table throughout the five weeks' voyage from Sydney to Southampton. With us, each evening, was a lovely auburn-haired Sydney girl, who had ambitions as a ballet dancer. Under the sky of the Pacific and Indian Oceans she would dance for Arthur and myself, at midnight, on the high 'D' deck; I can see her yet, luminous in the moonlight and, apparently, as immaterial. Arthur and I both fell for her. Always the three of us took coffee together after dinner. At Colombo, a young judge came aboard. And the girl left us to dance with him, 'just one dance', she explained. But she did not return; she danced with this young judge persistently. We waited. At last I said to Mailey: 'Arthur, let's go to bed. We'll teach her a lesson. She'll come back here for a drink, and find we've gone. Come.' Arthur agreed. So we departed to our own cabins, which adjoined. I waited till I heard Arthur's electric light click. I listened. Not a sound. After a while, giving him time really to get off to sleep, I crept up to the dancing deck. I stealthily tip-toed, watching the dancers through the window. Soon, surely, the dancing would come to an end. Then I would ... I saw her, still with the judge. Still, soon I would ... I turned the corner of the dance hall, in the outside dark. And I collided with Arthur. He too, had imagined he had heard *my* electric light click and thought I was safely asleep. He was the kind of blithe spirit that causes comical things like this to happen.

He took to cricket in the manner of nearly every Australian boy in his period of penniless nonage, playing with a kerosene tin for the wicket. At once he discovered that he could, with the sensitive education of his fingers, persuade a cricket ball to go through a kaleidoscope of changing curving flight and capricious gyrations from the earth; he could by spin and flight express his own mazeful mind. He was a romantic in the sense which is regarded as completely outmoded these days, a time of history described by Sir Thomas Beecham as 'the most barbaric since Attila'—and that is going back somewhat. Mailey when young was staggered one Saturday, in his head and his heart, to learn that he had been chosen to play in the first XI of his district 'Grade' contingent. (In Australia every suburban community has two or three cricket teams.) Moreover, young Arthur would, this very Saturday, be playing against Victor Trumper's side. And Victor then was in his prime, the idol worshipped by all Australian boys—and by English boys, myself included—the most chivalrous batsman of all time, the most gallant, versatile and youthful. His grave, in a churchyard outside Sydney, is to this day covered by fresh flowers. Young Mailey spent this Saturday morning, preceding the afternoon of his personal contact with Apollo, in an utter misery of anxiety. No; he wasn't worrying about his own likelihood or unlikelihood of performing ably in his baptism into top-class Sydney cricket, first rung on the ladder to Test matches. His concern was all for Victor—was he well, not afflicted by a chill? Would he get run over in the streets by a cab? People, sixty or so years ago, did somehow get run over by four-wheeled cabs, so Arthur's fears could be justified, considering the way God had made him, responsive to any romantic suggestion. Victor survived the morning's dangers; he did not cut himself dangerously while shaving, did not scald his hand with hot water, did not get run over in the streets. He played for his XI *v.* the XI containing the tyro Mailey. And Mailey couldn't believe it when his captain asked him *to bowl at Victor*! Arthur did bowl at the Incomparable. Victor enchanted Arthur by some strokes from his bowling which, Arthur remembered years after, were like strokes made by a bat of conjuration. Then, incredibly, Arthur clean bowled Victor. And, wrote Mailey, in his autobiography: 'I was ashamed. It was as though I had killed a dove.' Language to bring a blush to the cheeks of the latest of cricket's sophistical fellow-workers.

Mailey really was an incorrigible romantic. Throughout his life (and he passed his eightieth year), he remained, for all his show of worldliness, the poor boy of the Sydney slums, never stale at whatever life brought to him, always *experiencing* events with the boy's wonder—'how has all this happened to me?' On board ship, on his many voyages to England and back to Sydney, his crowning moments occurred whenever he gave a champagne cocktail party. Champagne, was for him, the symbol of the miracle which had changed him from a ragged urchin to one of the best-beloved and most magical of cricketers. He would often, in his cabin on the ship, listen to a gramophone record; Tauber singing about Vienna. He rented a flat in Park Lane during one of his summer visits to London. He gravitated naturally, on holiday, to Montmartre. He died happy. In his last moments of delirium, he imagined he was on board the Orient liner *Orion*, entertaining the ship's captain and officers to a champagne party. He squandered his imagination to the end, even as he tossed up his spin, with the millionaire's generosity. In heaven he has probably already clean bowled the Holy Ghost—with a 'googly'.

A Midsummer Day's Dream—
and Awakening

It really did all happen one day, in August 1935, at the Canterbury cricket Festival, sun-drenched from noon until half past six, that the players of Kent and Nottinghamshire walked into the field in deep pools of shadow. A military band played, and at eleven o'clock, just before the match began, life accidentally achieved for me a moment as of contrived art and hieratic benediction. I was standing in front of the memorial to Colin Blythe, the beautiful slow left-hand bowler of the 1890–1914 period who was killed in the war. The memorial is a simple drinking fountain, with these words inscribed on it: 'He was unsurpassed among the famous bowlers of his day and beloved by his fellow cricketers.' As I stood in the life-giving sunshine, nobody near me, but all around, not far away, the white tents, the happy bustle of the gathering holiday crowd, time as I felt it slipped back, and Blythe was bowling again for Kent, young in years and summers in plenty stored in him. He, the darling of Canterbury cricket Festivals was, in my mind's eye, still spinning the ball and curving it through the air to his heart's content on a high August noon as bounteous as this one. At this moment, as I looked at his memorial, and years fell away, and Blythe was happy and animate once more in my memory, the military band played the sad, simple air of Handel's 'Lascio chio pianga', music which tells of mortal yet blessed tears. For a moment my eyes could not see. Then the band struck up a gay tune, and the morning's brilliant multitudinous activity was resumed, laughter and the delusion of time-resistant human happiness brimming over in the endless sun. Larwood, at this point of his career, was reduced by some hurt to a foot to medium-pace; he ran to bowl with the merest hint of the aggressively accumulative gallop of his career's meridian, rhythmic but menacing. Batsmen now could resist his attack with some split seconds to spare; nonetheless, they needed to watch him carefully, for he was periodically capable of sudden combustion and spurts of explosive power, like a volcano mistakenly deemed extinct.

On this benign departed Canterbury afternoon, Woolley stole from the sunshine and incorporated into his batsmanship warmth and easy opulent rays, light and shade. Woolley was Kentish and Canterbury cricket in the flesh; so were Hutchings, Marsham, Valentine, Freeman, all apparently absorbed into the game, technique willing to wait on self-indulgent pleasure, in the season's weather.

'Tich' Freeman, bowler of leg-spin, was the Kent crowd's source of merriment when he came in to bat, not much taller than the crouching wicket-keeper. I see him now, this afternoon filched from the cricketer's paradise, attempting a mighty drive, missing the ball, whereat the military band broke into a polonaise by Chopin, warlike and aristocratic. There was also in this Kent *v.* Nottinghamshire match, in a Canterbury Festival as remote from our 1970s as the Canterbury Tales of Chaucer, a Nottinghamshire cricketer name of Harris, a determined passive resister with the bat, yet all the same intent on private personal amusement as he bent low and put to the bowlers a bat as though anaesthetic, rendering the nastiest ball more or less harmless and prone. He would, as he went in first for his county, arrive at the wicket, the game's opening stage, and address the opposition: 'Good morning, fellow workers.' He would proceed to stonewall for hours, anonymous, not there at all, except as the score-board registered, like a cash-desk, his score. Often I did not believe there was 'no such a person' as this Harris. He succeeded George Gunn as Nottinghamshire's No. 1 opening batsman; and nature believing that action and reaction are equal and opposite, created him as different from George Gunn, visually and internally, as Lucio is different, in Shakespeare, from Dogberry.

George Gunn was not always approving of military bands in action at cricket matches. When first he played for England *v.* Australia at Sydney, a band emitted strident sounds after the lunch interval. 'I was about 30 not out and that "googly" bowler Hordern was worritin' me,' he related. 'We didn't know much about "googly" bowlin' in those days. So I had to concentrate. Then the cornet in band got out of tune. And it took my mind off bowlin'. Cornet was flat all through "Brightly Dawns" in *Mikado*. It properly put me off; my mind was on that cornet; absolutely out of tune, all afternoon.' Gunn scored 62 while he was 'worritin'. It was George Gunn, who towards the end of his life, nearly eighty, arrived on a June day at Lord's, rolled umbrella, Savile Row suit. I saw him outside the Pavilion. 'I've just been in that pavilion Long Room,' he announced. 'But,' I said, 'you've been in the Long Room often enough?' 'No,' he explained, 'when I played, only amateurs were allowed in Long Room. We professionals had to stay in our own quarters. Well, I've just been in the Long Room. Only half-a-dozen members, all sittin' still, asleep.' He took me by the shoulder. 'Did you ever see that play called *Outward Bound*, where everybody on a ship was dead and they didn't know they were dead? That Long Room was like that. So I said to myself. "George, you'd better get out of it at once".' O, rare George Gunn, gone with the wind!

It is not a digression from the subject of Kent cricket to drag in George Gunn (in any case why should I not digress, as I compile my book? All good writing, and good talk, is digressive). In the 1930s Kent, in a fourth innings *v.* Nottinghamshire at Trent Bridge, collapsed before terrific bowling by Larwood, so that on a lovely afternoon—the closing afternoon of the match —Nottinghamshire needed to score only 140 or so, on a cushioned turf, with hours to spare. George Gunn and Whysall came forth to, as we imagined, collect these runs from Kent with condescending ease and leisure. The truth is that Gunn scored a hundred himself, in some ninety minutes. The match was finished, won and lost, at 5 o'clock; and the crowd had to leave the July field and go prematurely home. That evening I met Gunn, and asked him: 'Why the hurry this afternoon? You spoiled it for thousands, all sitting there happily.' 'Well,' he said, in his comfortable slow way, 'when we were coming downstairs from dressing-room, I asked Whysall, "Dodge, how many runs do we want to win?" and he said, "hundred and forty odd", so I said, "well, we'll share 'em 'tween us". Then, in pavilion, a member came up to me and said somethin' he shouldn't have, a Committee man. I can't tell you what it was he said, but it annoyed me, really; it made me right angry.' 'Yes, George,' I replied, 'but what's all this got to do with the hurry you were in to win the match?' 'That member,' said George emphatically, 'upset me so much that I had to take it out of Kent bowling.' The Kent slow bowler, 'Father' Marriott, played in this game. He assured me that Gunn cut late a medium-pace 'yorker' from him 'off the middle stump'. Marriott had a certain distinction as cricketer, beside that of being a great and studious student of spin; he was the least skilful batsman extant. In a single innings match, he bowled his opponent for 1—and lost it by an innings. This is by the way.

Not all cricket of yesteryear was bathed in sunshine, though memory would persuade you that it was. I recall a fearsome May day at Gloucester. A bitter wind blew down the wicket, from noon to arctic eve. Two spectators sat in it, facing it, hour after hour. In my report of the day's icy play, I commented upon the hardihood, the devotion to cricket, of these two frost-bitten spectators. But, I added, perhaps they were only dead. Torrents of sunshine in an English summer sometimes, then the rain, it raineth every day, with a Derby race run in a snow-storm. When I lived in Australia, young folk there usually hoped to go to London sooner or later; but they were rather afraid of an English winter. 'It's not the winter you should be anxious about,' I assured them, 'but the English summer.'

Absent from Leeds, 1929

At Leeds, July 13–16, 1929, a three-day Test match occurred: England *v.* South Africa. On the second evening, at close of play, the match seemed more or less finished, with South Africa defeated, seven wickets gone in their second innings, and only 24 ahead; moreover there was nobody left to defend one end of the wicket, only Quinn, Van der Merwe and Bell, none most days capable of surviving at all, as batsmen, against Tate, White, Freeman, Woolley, Hammond; for such was England's attack at Leeds in July 1929.

I decided to depart from Leeds on the evening of the second day of this now obviously completed Test match; there was only Owen-Smith likely to stay in next day for a few overs. I decided to go to London and spend a day in the country with Milady. Which I did. We wandered around Barnet; it was possible really to wander around Barnet in the summer of 1929. We arrived back in London, round about 6 o'clock. To my horror I saw an evening paper poster in Whitehall:

> ## SOUTH AFRICA'S
> ## GREAT RECOVERY

South Africa had indeed 'recovered' greatly. Owen-Smith had achieved the innings of his life, behind my back. Quinn, Van der Merwe and Bell had somehow been capable of long tenure at the wicket. South Africa had scored 275, and England, needing 184 to win, scraped home by 5 wickets, and might have lost but for an innings of 95 not out by Woolley.

I was in a nice mess. What could I do? The *Manchester Guardian* would be waiting for my 'from-the-spot' hot report. I had, of course, to dismiss Milady; no dinner together that evening. I rushed to my club and consulted the tape-messages reporting the bare details of the sensational third day's play in the Test match at Leeds. From these useful details and statistics, I composed a column of 'eye witness' descriptive writing. I then consulted the Bradshaw railway guide, saw that a train from Leeds arrived in London at about 9 o'clock, so I timed myself dramatically to rush into the office of the *Manchester Guardian* with my report. I reproduce it herewith:

'History has been made at cricket today in the burning heat of mid-summer. The South Africans kicked back from a position so hopeless that few of us even took the trouble to be present at Leeds until we scented the battle from afar, and then, by aid of all the modern arts of speed, and also by the aid of imagination, discovered ourselves once again in the cockpit. England contrived to win at the finish, but the moral victory belongs to South Africa.

'These young men from over the seas, who are here to learn cricket from the conquerors of Australia, have aimed a damaging blow at the reputation of some of our most notable players. Our bowling has been exposed as a thing of shreds and patches. For consider: on a dusty pitch, where even Woolley could turn the ball inches, South Africa's tail scored 159 for three wickets in about two hours. One of this "tail" was, of course, Owen-Smith, the young batsman described in these columns a month ago (after he had scored 25 at Birmingham) as the future Hobbs of South Africa. But Owen-Smith's colleagues at the wicket this morning were Quinn, Van der Merwe and Bell—three cricketers who themselves would not claim to possess more than elementary knowledge of the difficult art of batting. What are we to think of the English bowling that it could not get rid of three very modest batsmen cheaply on a dusty Leeds wicket? Owen-Smith played one of the greatest innings of Test match history, but at the other end of the pitch stood Quinn, Van der Merwe and Bell. And Bell, who is the least sophisticated batsman of the three, was given liberty to hold the last wicket while no fewer than 103 runs were added in little more than an hour. The lack of Larwood, injured, can only be stressed at risk of our dignity; there were Freeman, White, Hammond, Tate and Woolley, who, if they are good enough to bowl for England at all, ought to be good enough to account for the three last men of any South Africans' innings, at the fresh of the day. There was also the new ball at 200—and only Bell to overthrow with its notorious power. And Tate there to exploit it! It was left to Woolley to break this last-wicket stand. Later in the day Tate was lion-hearted at the crisis; he held his end while the incomparable Woolley won the match. Tate came in at a moment when it was torment to watch the match, let alone bat in it—torment for anybody not born a Woolley. Five wickets were down, and England still needed 74. But Tate's innings must not confuse the issue; he is supposed to be England's new-ball bowler. In this office he has been disappointing this year; he has worked too hard for England recently. Another new-ball bowler is urgently wanted.

'Owen-Smith and Quinn stayed in while South Africa's total went from 116 for seven to 168 for eight. Quinn hit Freeman to long-on for six. Owen-Smith attacked like Victor Trumper come back again to show us how quick feet, the trenchant bat, and the chivalrous heart can still make havoc of bowling, ancient or modern, spin, length, "googly", swerve. What stuff we have been told lately about the strange new subtleties that have entered into bowling this age! We have been told, too, that in Test cricket of the present time the field is set with a craftiness not known in the past. Owen-Smith, a lad of twenty, laughed out of existence these sophistries. He jumped to Freeman's spin—and where and what was the spin? At the boundary's edge, sometimes over it; stuff for brilliant batsmanship. He took command of the game the moment Bell came in, last of all. He manoeuvred so that he could get the bowling. And he enjoyed the bowling —that was the notable fact about his cricket.

'He reached his 50 in an hour and a half, in another 45 minutes he reached his 100. He made the highest score ever achieved in a Test match in this country by a South African, beating Catterall's 120 of 1924. He and Bell set up a South African record for the last wicket.

'Owen-Smith's batsmanship has for its technical foundation very mobile footwork. But footwork of agility springs from a brave and agile mind. The science of footwork is known intimately enough by most English batsmen—in the abstract. Unfortunately, few of them have the nerve to put it into practice. Owen-Smith jumped at Freeman with a ferocity that might have caused a greater bowler to quail; he hit him straight for so violent a six that the ball smote a stand and bounced back far onto the playing field. His cutting was as aggressive as his hitting in front of the wicket. Like every great batsman, he attacked the overtossed ball and then, when the bowler pitched short protectively, he cut. He sent a difficult return chance to Woolley with his score 67; he raised South Africa's innings to 200 by means of another six. When he was 92 he lifted a ball to mid-off; Goddard, substitute for Larwood, fell forward, and apparently held the catch for a second, but falling over, let go possession of it. The umpires ruled that it was not a catch. At 125 Owen-Smith gave another chance— this time to White at mid-off. To lay emphasis on these flaws would not be cricket. Indeed it was remarkable that a young batsman should have faltered so infrequently as this in an innings played at the speed of 129 in two hours and three-quarters. He hit two sixes and 15 fours. His instinct for the loose ball was unerring; in fact, he proved himself a great player in nothing quite so much as in his ability to make his own loose ball. There never was a great batsman who waited for bowlers to send easy balls.

'Owen-Smith's batting utterly lacks the modern characteristics. He does not face round to the bowler *before* he has seen what sort of ball is coming along. He does not deny himself a free lift-up of the bat. He does not let balls on the off side go by, and fling his bat over his shoulder and "pad-up" at the sight of them. If the ball is short, his right foot is thrust like lightning over the wicket and we see a square cut. If the ball is overtossed the left foot goes to it, and we see a drive. The movements of his bat flash in the sunshine, almost defying the eye to follow them. If it was safe at Birmingham last month to write of Owen-Smith as the successor to H. W. Taylor on the strength of 25 runs, it will be as safe today to describe him as one of the most gifted batsmen since cricket's golden age, which happened between 1900 and 1914.

'England's struggle to get 184 for victory would have been intolerable to watch had Woolley not been there to soothe and reassure us. Woolley's absence would have meant defeat for England. Sutcliffe and Hammond were out and only 13 up. A ball from Morkel rose sharply and Hammond put it into the air. Morkel dashed down the pitch and held the catch and turned a somersault. I have never before seen a team fling itself at all sorts and shadows of catches with the enthusiasm and alacrity of these young South Africans. Hereabout we were supposed to eat lunch. Bowley and Woolley pulled the match round by cricket so charming that our fears were actually shamed. In 65 minutes 85 were scored; then Bowley was caught trying a cut. Cricketers get out attempting cuts, true, but the game will not be great again until we encourage and trust the stroke as we did in other years. Bowley was out at 98. He has won his place in the England eleven. Panic sat up and shrieked once more when Hendren got out from a stroke which ended a short innings that will fix him in my mind for all time in the image of a human note of interrogation. The next ball saw Leyland play on. England were now 110 for 5. From his first ball, Tate was given the benefit of the doubt in an appeal for leg-before-wicket. Thereafter he proved himself a stout-hearted batsman who at the right moment can stifle an inborn desire for strokes across the line of the ball. For two hours and ten minutes Woolley played delicious cricket; the devil left the conflict at his sweet but strong command. He made batting seem so easy that it was really hard to believe that his side stood in any peril at all.

'The crowd cheered the South Africans for the heroes that they were. They won the day's laurels by play which rendered honour to cricket. Many victories have been won which have brought with them less glory than this very glorious defeat. In a period when we are witnessing too many matches played according to the Lancashire *v.* Yorkshire or the Notts *v.* Yorkshire plan, these South Africans are reminding us that cricket is a game with a tradition that has moved a Francis Thompson to immortal poetry. Tomorrow, and to the season's end, Deane shall have music wherever he goes; his team has won friends innumerable by today's gesture. . . .'

A fortnight later, during the Test match at Manchester, the South African captain, H. G. Deane, came to me to congratulate me on the account I had written in the *Manchester Guardian* about the great recovery at Leeds. 'You must have had the glasses on Owen-Smith all the time,' he said. The field-glasses of imagination. The point of this virtuoso report, written 200 miles 'from the spot', is that I knew how Owen-Smith batted; I had watched him carefully many times before he had played his superb 129 at Leeds, in my absence. I could at any moment, even now, write a fairly true description of, say, Kreisler playing the violin. The reader will note that in the bogus report from Leeds, the operative sentence is: 'The South African kicked back from a position so hopeless that few of us even took the trouble to be present at Leeds until we scented the battle from afar.' I admire yet the audacity of that sentence. Still, I do not reproduce my *tour de force* of journalistic resourcefulness as an example to all young reporters. It is safest and wisest to be, if not exactly geographically on the spot, at any rate adjacent.

MORE MUSIC-MAKERS

Klemperer

Klemperer, nineteenth-century musically conditioned and a Mahlerian, always remained apart from the obsessively romantic influences. He never wooed the impressionable senses in Bruno Walter's way; he was never soft-centred. In a talk with him he told me that though he admired Bruno Walter in general, he did not approve of his interpretations of Mahler. 'Too Jewish,' he said, with the right grimace. Like Furtwängler, Klemperer has constantly been a searcher, not satisfied with the sense-data of music, but intent on rooting out the core, the conceptual essence. But unlike Furtwängler the Faust in him, tirelessly renewing himself, has had at his shoulder the realistic Mephisto, adding the tincture of sharp-edged intellectual acidity to his fundamental view of music, a view as ethical at times as aesthetic. Beecham once described Klemperer as tone-deaf, a taunt with a grain of truth in it, because it is true that Klemperer is not interested primarily, or secondarily, in the orchestral palette as such. It is the absence in his conducting of sensuous indulgence, his acute understanding of proportion and directness of musical diction which enabled him to emerge from the nineteenth-century orchestral atmosphere in Germany to the more or less unromantic climate of our present day. Nonetheless, in his maturity he could weave spells enough, seducing the emotions or, rather, the religious instincts.

One Sunday morning in Vienna, Klemperer conducted the Ninth Symphony of Bruckner with the Philharmonic Orchestra. He was then an upright eagle of a man, masterful, somewhat inimical in looks. He stood before the orchestra on this September Sabbath in the Grosser Musikvereinssaal, arms outstretched, ready to begin the Bruckner symphony with a *fiat lux* imperative wave of his baton. He waited until the crowded hall was silent, baton poised. And a grey-haired Viennese sitting next to me leaned forward as though by magnetic attraction, and, before a note of Bruckner was sounded, buried his head in his hands and burst into tears. He was attending to Klemperer in the right spirit. Not that Klemperer is dominated by the notion of music as 'die heilige Kunst'. Amongst his own compositions is a 'Merry Waltz'. Moreover, his sense of humour is tart and barbed. Recently he asked Claudio Arrau: 'Have you heard Georg Szell's recording of Debussy's "La Mer"?' Arrau said he had not. And Klemperer gurgled: 'Szell am See, Szell am See.' The fact that Klemperer in old age is honoured as the most devout of Beethoven conductors should not lead us to forget that he once on a time was the pioneer of Schönberg, Hindemith and Stravinsky. As I say, at his shoulder, watching the natural romantic ethic core of Klemperer is 'der Geist der stets verneint', the denying spirit, quick to prick a pretentious bubble of emotion. Fischer-Dieskau sang his heart out in Bach's St Matthew Passion, prayerful, a singing 'deutsches Denkmal'. Klemperer, after the performance, or communion, went round to the artist's room and the Mephisto in him said to Fischer-Dieskau: 'Sie sollten Eisenstein singen.' A communion indeed of Bach and *Fledermaus*!

He has suffered violent physical assaults, a tumour on the brain, a broken femur, an escape from burning to death in bed. I have told him that his favourite symphony of Mahler should be the 'Resurrection'. If Klemperer today is regarded as a sort of prophet of Mahler, it is because, since Bruno Walter's passing, Mahler's music has been looked into from a different standpoint from that of Walter. The central psychology of Mahler, the bone of the matter, has been revealed. Klemperer removed the superfluous flesh, the *Schmalz*, from Mahler; for Mahler is not *all* heart-wringings of string portamento and appoggiatura. We need only to study the photographs of Mahler, the forehead from which the veins of intellect may almost be seen in pulsation. Every classic, said Stendhal, has been a romantic in his day. But, as I have argued, Klemperer's romanticism was never more than skin-deep. The orchestra, for Klemperer, is a medium, not an expressive entity in itself. He often seems to change the orchestral palette into a neutral grey. He is never the conscious Maestro; in fact, he has the classic secret of anonymity. His power over an orchestra works invisibly. Seated in a chair with his octogenarian immobility of limb, it would appear that once he has established the tempo, set the music into motion, it could proceed by its own volition, the instrumentalists moving on and on like the army of unalterable law. I have heard him set Mozart into motion with the simplest baton indication, and the patterns of tone have gravitated to their places in the musical sky as the stars in their courses.

Sir Thomas Beecham, who was antithetical to Klemperer in every way by mind, nature and general metabolism, regarded Klemperer, as I say, as tone-deaf. 'Thus,' spoke Sir Thomas, 'he is the ideal conductor of late and deaf Beethoven.' Klemperer's range of dynamic was always small, with no exaggerated pianissimi. His main asset has been a large-spanned grasp of a symphonic structure, the outlines, the rise and fall, as secure as those of a mountain range. He has tremendous will-power, the will to live and be Klemperer. In particular, he is master of the use of what I describe as the musical *colon*; in a Bruckner silence we hear, if we are listening with intelligent ears, the intake of breath, the 'Atempause'. No, it is not the intense, heartbreaking silence achieved by Furtwängler to which nerves and dramatic responses were stirred. In Klemperer's Bruckner the pauses are as overtones, telling us of the echoes remembered by Bruckner at play in the organ loft of St. Florian.

I am not going to belittle Klemperer here by praising him uncritically. There are vast tracks of music, great music, which are alien to Klemperer's musical sensitivity. I have heard him cause Mendelssohn to sound earthbound and aged. He is not happy with the *Lied von der Erde* of his beloved Mahler, or with Mahler's genial Fourth Symphony. Yet he has done necessary service to Mahler by revealing him to us as the keenest and closest thinker of all the late nineteenth-century symphonic composers.

To recall a phrase of the forgotten William James, Klemperer is one of the 'tough-minded'. Through fist-blows from fate strong and cruel enough to lay most mortals low, he came to fulfilment in and through Beethoven. In the prime of his life he had to be patient, waiting for fair recognition of his gifts. He was obliged to work in the shadow of Furtwängler, Toscanini, Walter. And in America his way of revealing or re-creating music was at the extreme of Toscanini's; indeed, it was at the extreme of the American tempo and colour of anything. He was 'discovered' for London by Walter Legge, the founder of the Philharmonia Orchestra—Walter Legge who has served music more generously, with more scholarship and truth than many of the art's renowned and decorated fellow-travellers. Klemperer gravitated to Legge no doubt in sympathy with an ironic, mischievous wave-length. One Saturday noon, an orchestra in London wanted to get away to a football match, but Klemperer continued to rehearse. So the first violin very deliberately consulted his wrist-watch. Klemperer took no notice, and began to conduct again. The first violin, after another fifty bars or so, consulted his watch with a more studied deliberation. No avail. So the first violin thrust his wrist-watch almost under Klemperer's nose, whereat Klemperer leaned forward, inspected the watch, and asked: 'Is it going?' At another rehearsal the drummer got into a rhythmic cul-de-sac. After receiving a curt censure from Klemperer, the drummer told him (and he came from the North of England): 'Look 'ere, Doctor Klemperer, I've been counting my bars for thirty years.' 'And how many have you counted so far?' growled Klemperer. This pointed tongue of Klemperer is seldom in evidence during his music-making. As I say, he is at bottom as much an ethical as a musical interpreter. His conducting almost tells us every time that he is a reader of Goethe. Few musicians have shared his simple, austere yet All-Fatherly stature. With Goethe he has had reason to say, many times: 'Nur der verdient sich Freiheit wie das Leben, der täglich sie erobern muss. . . .' Which is to say: 'He only is deserving of life and liberty who daily has to master both.'

Furtwängler

Furtwängler was for me an enigmatical conductor, spell-binding as he swayed us in *Tristan und Isolde*, ungenial—even intense—as he coped with *Die Meistersinger*. He was, of course, among conductors of his day one of the most magnetic. Ernest Newman would have none of him. Newman was obsessed by the 'objective truth' of a musical score and distrusted 'personal' interpretations or reactions. Newman put his faith in Toscanini, who, he maintained, saw and heard the score as in itself it really is. On one occasion, a concert of the Berlin Philharmonic Orchestra in the Queen's Hall in London, Newman during the course of an article confessed that, from his particular position in the hall, he could not follow Furtwängler's beat. I pointed out next day, in my report of the concert, that so long as the Berlin Philharmonic Orchestra was able to follow Furtwängler's beat, it scarcely mattered much if our most learned critic couldn't.

Furtwängler was at Toscanini's extreme, as man and musician. Toscanini, in his old age, seemed to aim at hunting down the 'Absolute', as though thinking: 'You do not want to hear *my* arbitrarily individual impressions of Beethoven. A score is definitive and fixed. It is my duty to read faithfully the composer's language, and to build a symphony much as any noble edifice is erected from the architect's blue-print. What would you think of a builder who allowed his personal reactions to interfere with a ground-plan, and altered shape, dimension and style of the structure because of some exultation or depression of his own emotional or sense responses?'

Furtwängler's reply to this theory conceivably might have taken this form: 'You are wrong, Maestro,' [supposing that any conductor has ever called another conductor 'Maestro'] 'you are wrong, even if admirable in your intentions. We are all, each and all of us, imprisoned more or less in our individual skins. My own philosophical training has taught me that it is a delusion to suppose we can, with much precision, perceive external truth, or the object as it really is. No two people agree entirely about the most palpable physical phenomenon, not even about the temperature in a railway carriage! How, then, can there possibly be final truths about an art so non-physical, so un-material, as music? Even the notation of music, the symbols by which the composers express themselves, mean little or nothing separated from their context. You cannot compile a dictionary of crotchets, quavers, minims. Music is essentially a language *per se*, an art of suggestion to the emotions, mind and aural sense; it can be presented only as it is felt or perceived by the interpreter at the moment of performance. His only intellectual responsibility is to style, which, let us hope, he has learned to grasp by historical study and perpetual absorption in all sorts of music. He must not allow Mozart's pulse to beat with the blood and tensions of Beethoven's period. In all music, the conductor is bound to be something of an actor, capable of dramatising the different composers. He cannot stand apart from them. He is not in the withdrawn position of the chemist who said to the Royal personage: "The elements will now have the honour of combining in the presence of your Majesty".' (I apologise to the shade of Furtwängler for the flippancy of that closing sentence in a statement imaginatively attributed to him; but I couldn't resist it.)

For Furtwängler, the printed score was not a final statement. It was more than that; it was a complex of signs or symbols— and a starting-point. He attended as scrupulously as Toscanini to the notes as written down in black and white during the lifetime of the composer; but he sought to deduce, by emphasis on this or that feature of harmony, phrasing, rhythm and whatever, what the underlying conception could have meant as a mode or modes of consciousness in the creative forge itself. Furtwängler lived into an epoch which, reacting against egoistic and emotionally charged readings of the classics, insisted on an effort *objectively* to apprehend the score. The fact is, of course, that Toscanini and Furtwängler were both 'in the right', from different points of aesthetic view. I cannot understand the school of music criticism, or of musicology, which argues that there is only one view of, or reaction to, say, Beethoven's Ninth Symphony. We do not demand that all actors should agree on one, and only one, 'objective' interpretation of Hamlet. Is music a science limited for ever to a settled order? Is it unable to survive many imaginative imputations? And has it not a plastic means of signification related to an expanding way of life and thinking? Weber once said words to this effect, concerning the interpretation of music: 'The meaning can be found only in an understanding human heart; and if this feeling is lacking, a metronome cannot help us. And the score is no help either. . . .'

Furtwängler repudiated every schematic pattern of interpretation. A rehearsal with Furtwängler was not a polishing or varnishing, preparatory for public presentation. 'The essentials of a performance', he declared, 'cannot be determined in advance.'

He was a thoroughly equipped musician who was, I think, sometimes unable to realise the whole of his creative energy by means of interpretation. He ached to create first-hand, to compose. His symphonies are comprehensive, urgent and—as Moritz Rosenthal might have said—written from memory. In his conducting he appeared to venture too far into the creative smithy, so to say, there to liberate himself from frustration as he indirectly collaborated with an authentic creative genius. Toscanini regarded the orchestra much as a sculptor regards his inanimate material. The statue is in the block waiting for the artist to discover it and release it from its surrounding, transient and superfluous stuff. Furtwängler, so it seemed to me, sought to go into an orchestra to stir up sleeping fires, stir into combustion sluggish coal. His musical aesthetic was, naturally enough, post-Wagnerian or near-Wagnerian; he was always fertilising music with his own dramatic, even ethical, connotations. His faults were the consequence of his great traits. His conducting of *Tristan und Isolde* was a penetration not only to the brain, but the nerve centres. The pauses he risked at the beginning of the Prelude to Act I caused me, at first hearing, to think something had gone wrong in the submerged orchestral pit. Then, in the silences, we could hear the heart of the music beating; and the music drama went to its end, the end foreseen in the beginning, —'ohne Hast aber ohne Rast'.

Furtwängler's interpretations had a wide range of shading. He could obtain a pianissimo resembling silence just audible. His variety of expression was usually highly-strung, even neurotic. But the shot-silk beauty of his conducting of *Tristan* I hope never to forget; the unforced yet, paradoxically, throbbing passion of it, with the 'Liebestod' burning at the end a sad rather than tragic flame. He was a tall, lean man, with a high forehead, deep-set eyes, a thin sensitive mouth, a long neck and narrow sloping shoulders. A current of nervous energy apparently passed through him. After a spasmodic gyration of his baton, to liberate a work, his body swayed as though the music were conducting *him*; now his baton was a painter's brush, yielding and malleable. The difference between him and Toscanini—the comparison was constantly being made during Furtwängler's closing decade—could most forcibly be put by comparing the two artists' treatment of the second movement of Beethoven's 'Pastoral' Symphony. Toscanini took to the country air riding in a handsome stream-lined car; he listened to the murmurings of the brook from a civilised, not to say Rolls-immaculate interior; a map of the district was at hand. Furtwängler roamed the meadows—as Beethoven himself did —his breast only momentarily rested. He was a sort of Werther of his time; or a Faust who lacked the ironic corrective of a Mephistopheles.

Schwarzkopf, Fischer-Dieskau and Legge

It is the irony of things that we are praised for the achievements which come to us the easiest way; in fact, they are not achievements at all; in such moments of easeful production and performance we are vouchsafed grace, the creative or interpretative bowels move by divine freedom of will or relaxation. The test is when we have to win through by intelligence, and by a professional craftsmanship. The gifted amateur can do well when in the mood; the professional cannot, by reason of a technique which is experienced, fall below a certain level of performance or production.

These solemn thoughts are prompted by recollection of a recital some years ago by Elisabeth Schwarzkopf in the Royal Festival Hall in London. At the last minute she was called to fill the place of Fischer-Dieskau, suddenly taken hoarse. A different programme was, of course, arranged. To stiffen the challenge, or ordeal, before Schwarzkopf on this occasion, she was vocally tired; and the pianist to play, as she sang, was not Gerald Moore, with whose mind and fingers she was entirely happily related, larynx and sensibility; the piano for her now was played by Joerg Demus.

The pressure on singer and pianist could be felt for some time, as it could be felt by the artists themselves, exposed on a platform in a curiously inimical atmosphere to begin with. 'Substitute' artists and programmes always start from a sense of disappointment in the audience and a fluctuating expectation of compensation for anticipated pleasures frustrated. Schwarzkopf's charm of presence could not thaw a rather frosty air as she and Demus sought to evocate 'An die Musik' of Schubert, which came to us statically, ready-made, out of stock, a kind of 'prepared' Schubert. 'Der Einsame' was presented by Schwarzkopf not so much sung as enunciated, by means of flexible speech-song—'Der Einsame', the solitary one, addressing an audience. The temperature of the concert fell even lower.

Then the miracle of recovery, or rather of self-mastery by Schwarzkopf. In songs by Hugo Wolf, all *Wilhelm Meister* settings, the artist and the professional in her coped with the so far barren musical environment. Wolf does not demand, as Schubert unselfconsciously does, a natural tone and unimpeded phrasing, phrasing with no accentuation which is not part and pulse-beat of a musical phrase itself. In Wolf, the instinct for the dramatic or the histrionic is almost as important as the actual vocal quality. 'Heiss mich nicht reden', 'Nur wer die Sehnsucht kennt', and 'So lasst mich scheinen', were each superbly incorporated by Schwarzkopf into soul and body of her. Mignon's character was vividly suggested by tone and extraordinary understanding of verbal nuance. The recital became truly memorable by her interpretation of 'Kennst du das Land'. In this great song, Wolf goes beyond the psychological stature of the pathetic child of the novel. The music fully takes the measure of Goethe's self-revealing poetry which, knowing or not, he infused into his creation of Mignon, a poetry transcending the immediate object of the novelist in him, and calling back poignant emotions and memories of the 'Italian Journey'. Altogether this concert, one of a hundred I have attended over the past decade, remains for me an 'experience'.

Schwarzkopf has always had at her command much more than allurement of presence on a concert-platform; she has consistently been a singer of rare range of culture and musical acuteness and awareness. The remarkable fact about the impressions she has made on me is that few have been imprinted on memory in the opera house, where by mischance I have seldom heard or seen her. Yet she has, by personal gift of histrionic suggestions, deluded me at times to imagining that I have *seen* her portrayal on the stage of Hanna in *The Merry Widow*, of Madeleine in *Capriccio*; yet it is by gramophone records alone that she has caused these wonderful illusions. I have not even seen her incomparable Donna Elvira except in a concert version, an Elvira stationary, in evening dress; nonetheless, she spell-bound me to the belief that there has not been witnessed in any opera house a more completely 'realised' Elvira than Schwarzkopf's, a desperate, pursuing, strongly passionate, yet pathetically broken and clinging creature.

I have known admirers of Schwarzkopf who have argued that naturally and really she is, or was, born to be a singer on the lyric, even the operetta plane, and have referred to her enchanting realisations of Massenet's Manon and Lehár's Hanna as proof of this contention. These admirers have maintained that she was 'made' into a Wolf interpreter by the guidance of her husband, Walter Legge. I, who not only admire Schwarzkopf but have affection for her, can see the point of this view of her art and of the shaping of it; but I think she has so much musical intelligence of her own that she could have herself found the way. The probability is that Legge has directed, rather than coached her. The one serious limitation I find, or feel, in her singing is a certain recurrent self-consciousness. For example, she *identifies* herself with Strauss's Marschallin rather than *participates*, so that we are momentarily aware of Schwarzkopf. Lehmann lived *in* the body and mind of the Marschallin; indeed, so much so that often the Marschallin followed her into other realms of opera. Her Ev'chen in *Die Meistersinger* might well have been the Marschallin's younger sister. I once went so far as to describe a Lieder recital by Lotte as a recital by the Marschallin. It is a compliment to Schwarzkopf's suffusing personal presence that she cannot easily subdue it to her capacity for dramatic representation.

She has been fortunate, of course, to come under the cultural influence of Walter Legge, whose knowledge of German Lieder, and of opera in general, is not many times surpassed for swift imaginative insight. I have known Legge since he worked for His Master's Voice in the Clerkenwell Road. He was the first man to put recording on a basis appealing to serious musicians. He fought hard with H.M.V.'s directors to get published the

famous 'Society' albums of records of the early 1930s; the Hugo
Wolf album, and so on. We met in the lamentably gone Pagani's
restaurant in Great Portland Street, the restaurant of one's
dreams, where dined Caruso, Toscanini, Kreisler and the rest of
the legendary ones. One evening Legge, then in his mid-twenties,
vowed to me that one day he would 'create the best orchestra in
England, marry the most beautiful opera singer in Europe,
and direct a great opera house'. So far, he has attained two of
these ambitions. During the Hitler war, he was virtually the
benevolent dictator of musical activity in bomb-stricken
London. Somehow he allowed the ball to roll away from his
feet twice. The Philharmonia Orchestra, at its maturest, passed
from his control. His control of music in an important recording
channel was also lost. Few men have contributed as richly as
Legge to the formation of a deep-rooted and tasteful musical
and cultural life in London. His Philharmonia Concerts never
lapsed into routine; every programme he presented had in
it style and appeal to the civilised ear and eye. He more or less
re-discovered Klemperer for London. Klemperer, as I have
recorded, was not easily taken to heart or mind of London
music-critics. Legge's faith in Klemperer was strongest at a
time critical, a time of physical assaults on Klemperer.

Legge, a Wagnerian, has, like most Wagnerians, had in him
something of Wagner's dichotomy of psychology. He was, as
administrator and artist, possessed by an uncompromising
idealism; he never corrupted or dishonoured music; he gave
the whole of his intelligence and ambition to music, and was
ruthless to anybody who backslided, no matter how highly
esteemed he or she may have been by the public as a performer,
or by his or her agent. He would not tolerate a hint of tasteless-
ness, or a hint of weakness of artistic conscience. Naturally, he
made enemies; from his more than humanly normal zeal for
artistic perfection, inevitably there were reactions—his everyday
self could not live up to the perfectionist. As a man—and I
write of him as a friend of many years standing (or survival)—
he could be trying to one's code of manners. His tongue was,
from time to time, wounding and disrespectful, even banal in
its verbal caricatures of not present company. 'Nobody really

likes me,' he once said to me, 'you see, *I* am a Mephistopheles!'
'Yes, Walter,' I retorted, 'Gounod's.' And he was the first to
answer me: 'Touché.' I was perpetually being surprised at this
mingling in him of lofty-mindedness, of a quite rarefied though
broad culture, with a certain provincial complacency and
familiarity. His culture, *au fond*, was German, by assimilation
rather than European. That accounts for much in Walter's
psychological make-up.

It is probable, if not certain, that it was because of the
pioneer work of Legge, Schwarzkopf and Fischer-Dieskau
through the medium of gramophone, that a near miracle happened in the 1950s—the Royal Festival Hall packed for a concert of songs, all by Hugo Wolf. Gerhardt could lure large
audiences to listen to Schubert, but not exclusively to Wolf,
whose Lieder were hardly known in this country until Newman
wrote about him, not musicologically, not instructing us that
he modulated into such-and-such a key, from such-and-such a
key, but presenting him as a living voltaged human dynamo of
Lieder, transforming his reactions to the visible universe into
sound, tones vocal and pianistic.

If I had to choose again for my memories a few carefully
selected impressions to take with me to my desert island, unhesitatingly I would wish recalled a Wolf recital of some couple
of decades ago in London—the artists Schwarzkopf and Fischer-
Dieskau. Legge did not, I think, introduce Fischer-Dieskau to
London; Beecham was the first of our concert administrators to
bring him here and, of all music, to sing in Delius's *Mass of Life*
in which Fischer-Dieskau did sing the baritone (Zarathustra)
part from memory—a generous act of absorption, because
Fischer-Dieskau must have known when he accepted Beecham's
invitation to take part in the performance that the chances he
would again, for years, sing in the Delius *Mass* were all Lombard
Street to a China orange.

At the Wolf recital I am at this moment revisiting in tranquil
recollection, the two books of the 'Italian' songs were sung with
a pianist, so I guess, named Reuter. It is easier for a man than a
woman to get into the necessary trance-like intensity while in-
terpreting the 'Italian' songs (something of the trance-like inten-

149

sity in which Wolf composed then); for many of those written for the man's voice are rapt or contemplative, as the beauty of the beloved is extolled. But the woman, or women, in Wolf's 'Italian' songs, are volatile of mood, sometimes vixenish, mocking, ironical, even inclined to coyness.

Schwarzkopf conveyed to me every swift flash of eye and of temper, wit and passion. Then, as soon as the piano whipped or flicked a song to its end, the voice having finished its say, the light of imaginative participation seemed cut off in the singer's mind; her face became an impersonal mask. Lines of communication between singer and audience were broken and, by piano coda alone, Wolf was making his summing-up comment undisturbed. There was in Schwarzkopf's presence, radiantly though it was 'produced', none of that familiarity of singer with audience which disperses illusion—but encourages applause.

I have not consistently remained in sympathy with Fischer-Dieskau. Many times he has sounded in my ears, and appeared before my vision, as too German, making even Schubert sound German, unsmiling and—God bless the mark and forgive me— egoistical. Schubert egoistical! Du lieber Himmel!

At this cherished concert, Fischer-Dieskau could well have been singing under Wolf's personal hypnotism; he was like a *medium*, suggesting that his own consciousness had been withdrawn, or taken by Wolf into Wolf's world for Wolf's consuming purpose as he stood before us, eyes closed at times, and now and again intoning a soft phrase so breathlessly that the notes could be heard mainly by imagination's ear.

There was his sigh, on the falling seventh on the word 'letzte' in 'Herauf dein blondes Haupt'; I hear the echo of it in the magic sea-shell of memory; I hear also Fischer-Dieskau's majestic swell of tone in 'Gesegnet sei', at the words, 'Er schuf das Paradies mit ew'gem Licht'—'He created paradise with eternal light';—and the ensuing pianissimi, a sudden hush of awe and devotion, as he sang the exquisite and poignant closing line: 'Er schuf die Schönheit und dein Angesicht'—'He created beauty and thy face'. Such art enhances our material lives momentarily; by it we become vessels of grace—momentarily, as I say.

The pianist, of course, in a Wolf song is as responsible a collaborator as the singer. The truly reliable Wolf pianists of recent years have been Hermann Reuter, who played for Schwarzkopf and Fischer-Dieskau on the past occasion I am now trying to conjure back to the present; and, needless to say but it must be said, Gerald Moore. In passing, though, I might mention that, as far as these British Isles are concerned, Moore was not the first accompanist to break free of platform servitude to vocal soloists; Ivor Newton led the way from captivity for his kind. I imagine that one of the most difficult piano passages in all Lieder to play with the necessary touch and suggestive softness of tone are the arpeggio chords in Wolf's setting of 'Und willst du deinen Liebsten', calling up scene and distance for us, as the music tells of the threadlike beauty of the girl's hair—'Goldfäden, Seidenfäden'. Lovely words; and the pity is that we have lived to endure an age in which poets close their minds against language so romantically enchanting.

Schwarzkopf has intermittently irritated me by taking an audience into her confidence, to the extent of risking parody from Joyce Grenfell. Wolf disciplines her. She can incomparably convey the raptness, and also the witty clinch, of 'Du denkst' and 'Ich bin verliebt doch eben nicht in dich' of the song 'Wir haben beide'. So easily can this clinch of final phrases, even in Wolf, end in a sort of musical and vocal smirk. Coyness should be avoided at all costs. In general, Schwarzkopf treats the recurrent implications of coy confidentiality in Wolf by drawing on the inflections of recitative or *Sprechgesang*, pointing these inflections with her own witty relish. The play of expression on her face is as though rippled by Wolf's music; and it does not hint of the by-play known as 'character acting'. The music of Wolf prompts her, animates her, and so she becomes, more and more, the blissful Wolf *recording* angel. When we hear Wolf sung by artists dedicated to him, we are shaken to the heart by a possessed genius's creative agonies, agonies of rapture, torment, faith and consuming despair as creator, fruitful one season, frozen to ice another. We don't deserve the earthly visitations from these artists with a *daemon* in their bosoms, who crucify themselves to give beauty to a world which increasingly seems able to get on without it, changes the nature of it to a commuter, computer two-way traffic; artists crucified with no hope of a resurrection placing them in a front seat on the right hand of the All-Father.

EROTICISM IN ENGLAND

English women have assured me that it is only out of England —in France, Italy or Austria—that a woman is made aware that she is indeed a woman; not in England. On the Continent men look twice at a pretty woman. A friend of mine's daughter, eighteen years old, went alone to Rome for a summer holiday. She was obliged to return to the safe-conducted purlieus of Ealing after a week in the Holy City. She was pursued by young Italians; they looked at her—but not the package tourists from England—as though she were one of the 'sights', one of the spectacles of Rome. She is able to walk unobserved down London's Oxford Street.

I do not regard the 'swinging' sex obsessions of London's 1970s as erotic; they have as much to do with romantic and civilised sexual passion as pills, drugs, guitars and the erotically respectable wailings of the Beatles and the Rolling Stones. There is little, if any, erotic English poetry or music. No doubt there are hundreds of English songs and verses which deal more or less lyrically with devotion of man to woman, of lad to lass, of affection, of heart-to-heart responses between the sexes, of spiritual courtship and domestic wedlock, of regret, innocence betrayed, and tears, idle tears. My contention is that eroticism in our music and poetry, especially in our music, is hard to seek; I mean a music which springs uninhibitedly from an emotional experience embraced without reserve, and remembered with not too much tranquillity, then expressed with freedom, joy and pride. English love-music is self-conscious, as self-conscious as most English men and women (of all ages) while supposedly they are going through the first careless raptures. A moral censor is at hand, invisible but nonetheless felt to be present and watching. Passion, if we can use so strong a term in this context, is placed by our composers in a moral, a social scene. This argument is settled, as far as I am concerned, simply by asking if by any stretch of imagination we can conceive of an English *Tristan und Isolde*. Or can we see or hear any English composer getting out of his system a song as romantically insinuating as Wolf's 'Geh' Geliebte', or songs of the mysterious phallically evocative world of Debussy's 'Chansons de Bilitis'? Imagine an English 'West-Oestlicher Divan'! In English opera, there is no hint of a Carmen, a Tosca, a Manon, not even a Zerlina. In the one full-scale English opera, as I regard it, *Peter Grimes*, the driving creative force is that which makes sea and town gossip the determining protagonists. No Don Giovanni would write the name of Ellen in his list. In Tippett's *The Midsummer Marriage* the love music is idyllic or respectably symbolical; there is no erotic urge here taking risks.

There is, of course a whole anthology of English songs and poems which from their titles and words come into the category I am now talking about; but none is entirely free of the puritan impediment, or without evidence of a restrained sensuousness, a restrained emotional participation. The sense of secrecy is missing from English love-music and poetry (even Byron, in 'Don Juan', is colloquial and, so to say, un-private). As a people, we relate the arts to a 'committed', social awareness today more than ever before in our island's history. When all is said, and all has been twanged and bowed, the only genius of 'light' music produced in England has been the Irish Sullivan's; and he *is*—whatever belittlement of him issues from Hampstead and the mews of Chelsea—something of a genius, above talent. Nonetheless, his wit and appeal were in tune with English middle-class environment and consciousness of his period. There is no 'sex appeal' in Sullivan. If the senses are titillated by Sullivan at all, it is with an eye on the respectability of the English family group. The inhibition did no harm to a composer born to animate the comedy of Gilbert; all the same, the echo of the

Chapel Royal is recurrent throughout the Savoy operas. And I am not one of Sullivan's or Gilbert's 'superior' detractors.

It is possible that I am using the word erotic in a particular and not a generally applied way. Nobody would argue that there is much of eroticism in Brahms, yet he composed love songs well and warmly enough. But they express, I think, an elderly avuncular attitude to passion, with cosily sentimental implications. There are, indeed, great love-poems and love-music not fairly to be called erotic. After his Italian journey, Goethe wrote the 'Roman Elegies' in which emotion primarily erotic has been drawn through the sieve of masterful self-control and objectivity. All the same, the absorption in a sexual experience and pleasure can be felt pervasively in these poems. In one of the 'Roman Elegies', Goethe can, without lowering the temperature, tell us that while he lay with his beloved, he counted on her back the hexameters of the poem he was already writing for her as she slept the sleep of love and her warm breath went into his being. In the English view, there might seem something faintly comic about the notion of a poet composing hexameters in these circumstances. It is, though, because English composers, and not a few English poets, do not give themselves wholly to an erotic theme that they fail to create an impression of rapturous yet secretive abandonment. As in our music, there are in English poetry countless things said beautifully or prettily about love—*about*, but not *in* love. A poem such as Byron's 'So we'll go no more a-roving' is rare from an Englishman. Certainly few songs by English composers fit in with my idea of the erotic, or imply the absorbed passionate creative state which gives us almost the impression, or experience at second hand, of an act of *aesthetic coition*, when the artist's imagination embraces a recollected physical ecstasy. The inhibitions may be the consequence of puritanism bred long ago, or of our climate, or of our food; it is hard to say. Eroticism is not, of course, absolutely essential to the power and urge of musical creation; but it is useful if the composition of a love-song is in view. Beethoven composed powerfully enough without aid of eroticism; and he happened to be a full man and no less, not wanting red corpuscles. Very few composers, in fact, have produced vital and lasting music that is without passion, without a kind of tonal libido, which might easily have surged into the erotic canal. Elgar's music is not erotic; nonetheless, *Gerontius* has an intensity of mind and emotion charged beyond the adolescent mental reactions of most contemporary music, English or other.

I here am tempted to remark, not entirely irrelevantly to our present theme concerning the influence of the erotic in our music, that recently English composers have given to the stage a whole crop of operas—*Peter Grimes*, *The Midsummer Marriage*, *Lord Nelson*, et cetera, yet we still, as a nation, have no songs which do not turn pale heard immediately after, say, the 'Nuits d'Été' of Berlioz. Myself, I have been bold enough to produce from my not entirely British system or metabolism a 'Kitsch' waltz, which I herewith present to public view for the first time; words and music all mine own:

LOVE ME, LOVE ME
Waltz Song
Words and music by Neville Cardus

Opus 1 (!)

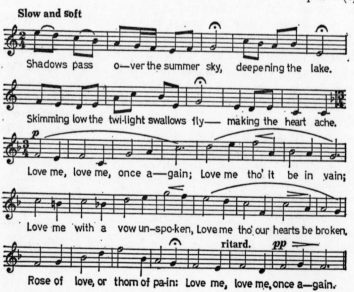

As far as I can remember, only Noël Coward of home-grown music-makers has conjured from his middle-class consciousness a tune, a waltz that aspires to the condition of 'Kitsch'. So does mine.

AUSTRALIAN YEARS

To Paula

During the late summer of 1939, when war with Hitler was a pretty certain fulfilment, I found that my two occupations had gone. I was then living in Manchester, working for the *Manchester Guardian* as music-critic and writer on cricket. I was half-way to my fifty-first year. The Free Trade Hall, in the city of my birth, home of the Hallé Concerts, was appropriated at once by the army authorities; for months now, music-making in public places came to a natural pause, excepting on casual afternoons in London, and at the historic chamber concerts in the National Gallery. As far as I was concerned I counted amongst the unemployed in Manchester. Frankly I could not continue, with any self-respect, to go on drawing my *Manchester Guardian* salary without returning it, as I had returned it for more than twenty years, with interest. Moreover, I could not pretend that physically or mentally my presence in the 'Services', or as part of the 'War Effort', would contribute to the nation's and the Empire's military advantage, as offensive or defensive participant. I suffered acute unhappiness. My wife, an art teacher at a school, accompanied evacuated children. The blackouts of the 'phoney' war encircled everybody in gloom, especially those of us who were, by choice, age or bodily necessity, made temporarily superfluous, socially and militarily.

I travelled to London in August, just before Hitler marched into Poland, to see what was destined to be my last view of a cricket match at Lord's for another eight years. Balloon barrages hovered in the sky; war was imminent. A ghostly county fixture was proceeding, Middlesex *v.* Warwickshire. Nobody was present to watch it, excepting a few elderly faithfuls. There was no legal way of stopping the match; it simply had to go on. Now happened the incident I have described elsewhere. Nobody has believed that actually it did happen, yet it is true. I looked at this spectral cricket match through the windows of the Long Room, my only company a vintaged M.C.C. member, white moustache, Eton tie, starched wing collar. In those days we didn't speak in the Long Room to anybody not formally introduced. Two working men entered the Long Room at this moment of crisis in the history of Lord's and of the outer world. They carried a green bag. They took down the bust of W. G. Grace from its pedestal and placed it in the green bag—security precautions in case of air raids. The vintaged M.C.C. member touched me on the shoulder, introduction or no introduction, and said: 'Did you see that?' I told him I had seen it. '*That* means war,' he affirmed.

A week or two afterwards, I heard my last concert in London for nearly a decade. Beecham conducted in the Queen's Hall one afternoon. Bombs were expected every evening, at sunset. I recall this concert mainly because it began with the National Anthem, which a standing audience sang fervently—none more fervently than a Hitler refugee, more English than the English, as he vociferously enunciated 'Gott safe ower gracious König . . .' On my return to Manchester, a city of the past for me already, a cable was waiting me, a bolt from the blue, a cable from Sir Keith Murdoch, newspaper tycoon in Melbourne; in Australia they called him 'Lord Southcliffe'—a kind of Antipodean Northcliffe! Sir Thomas Beecham was on his way to conduct in Australia, and Murdoch invited me to cover the Beecham tour for his chain of newspapers. So, in early January 1940, I flew by flying boat to Australia, to join the staff of the *Melbourne Herald*, an evening publication, as music-critic. I intended to return to England in three months at the end of the Beecham cavalcade. I stayed in Australia until 1948. My wife followed in 1941. But I did not stay in Melbourne. I could not write about music in an evening paper. I asked Murdoch to release me from an unwritten agreement, which he did, characteristically understanding. Nearly broke, I flew one Saturday to Sydney, offered myself to the *Sydney Morning Herald* as music-critic, and gladly agreed to the terms of five guineas weekly. There was plenty of music in Sydney to keep me busy, three or four nights a week. I was also asked by the Australian Broadcasting Commission to give a talk about music every Sunday, lasting an hour. I began with popular stuff, then risked Mahler's *Das Lied von der Erde*. At the close of this talk I could not get away from the recording studio for half an hour. From all over the continent came telephone calls of quite touching appreciation of the music, many, of course, from men and women driven to Australia by Hitler; but as many calls were from Australians, one from, of all distant places, Alice Springs. Something in *Das Lied von der Erde* sought out a deep spot in Australia's fundamental loneliness.

I naturally hoped to make a good impression by my first concert notice in the *Sydney Morning Herald*; so imagine my despair when I learned that the programme of my baptism as music-critic in Australia was as hackneyed as this (or some such): the *Oberon* Overture of Weber, an early Schubert symphony, and Beethoven's Fifth. What could I possibly write, with a fresh urge, about music so familiar? As a fact, the concert was for me an illumination and living proof that there are no hackneyed masterpieces, only hackneyed critics. The audience listened to all this old 'established' music exactly as I had listened to it in my salad days. Music was not so common an occurrence in Sydney, thirty years ago; it couldn't be turned on at home like the bath tap. In Sydney I, hard-bitten critic of music, was able to put myself to school again, to hear music with susceptibilities renewed by contact with listeners unstaled. Moreover, I soon realised that music-criticism in Australia was a responsible job; I could do good, and I could do great harm. In London so many expert writers about concerts are proliferating every day; they cancel out one another's opinions. Besides, standards of taste and of judgment are pretty well fixed in Europe, subject though they may be to whims of fashion. In Sydney, I quickly realised that I was a sort of gardener in the field of music, plucking out a weed here, or tending a delicate and promising growth there. Most of the weeds, to begin with, were English transplantations. I had to remove from professorial or teaching positions one or two importations from London, notably a whole caterwaul of so-called 'principal tenors' from Covent Garden Opera, quite unknown to me.

A controversy was in full spate in the correspondence columns of the *Sydney Morning Herald* about the use of German in the coaching of Lieder at the local Conservatorium of Music (yes, they call it a Conservatorium in Sydney; that is, when they don't call it just the 'Con'). One professor wrote in to the paper stating he would never dream of instructing his pupils to 'pronounce the language employed by Hitler'. I wrote a letter to the paper pointing out that Goethe had also pronounced much the same language, and anyhow he, the professor, was not himself exactly proficient in German. Another teacher, a woman, also announced in print that on principle she would not coach her students in German while Hitler was alive to speak it. A few days after her letter had seen the light, I chanced to be giving a broadcast. This patriotic lady was herself giving a recital of German Lieder even as I waited for my turn in an adjoining studio, where I could hear her singing Wolf and Schubert in English. When she had finished her recital and had come from the microphone studio through the room I was waiting in, I congratulated her: 'So glad you've stopped all that nonsense about the language of Hitler and have decided to sing German Lieder in German.' She was, needless to say, indignant. 'But I *was* singing in English,' she snorted. In time we became friends, but not for a long time.

I enjoyed myself vastly. Taxi-drivers, taking me from the concert-hall to the office of the *Herald*, would ask me: 'Well, Mr. Cardus, are you givin' 'em 'ell agen ternight?' But I am in error in saying that I was driven by taxi to the *Herald* office; no, my destination after a concert was always the General Post Office in Martin Place. It was there I wrote my concert notices during my seven years as music-critic in Sydney. I was shy about going into the office of the *Herald* late at night, where the staff could be distractingly voluble. The men behind the counter of the Sydney G.P.O. at first were concerned as they saw me

standing up, scribbling away. 'If it's a cable, it's goin' to cost
you the earth.' They were highly collaborative and friendly
when informed of the fact that I was not adding heavily to their
late night duties. One of them said: 'We'll have a plaque put
up—"Neville Cardus wrote here!".' In recent years the *Sydney
Morning Herald* has moved to a new office, and it is all stream-
lined and efficient; concealed lights for the reporters, every
convenience. Angus McLachlan, who edited my notices with
an economical eye on my semi-colons, made an inaugural speech
at the opening of the new *Herald* premises; referring to the
latest gadgets and whatever, pointing out at the same time that
the best writing ever to appear in the paper had been done
standing upright at a public desk in the G.P.O. I recount this
compliment unblushingly, with pride and a good laugh, accompanied by an acute ache of nostalgia for those very good days.

The quality of musical performances in Australia was naturally variable. War demands had taken away from the orchestras
many expert instrumentalists. Nonetheless, concerts abounded
in Sydney, with always the likelihood that some budding talent
would attract the gardener's attention. It was in Sydney I performed my famous hat-trick of critical opinion. Each Wednes-
day I gave a broadcast to children, a ten minutes' talk with
gramophone records. This talk was preceded by one, also for
children, on drama. A young Australian did the 'effects', rattling
coconuts to depict galloping horses, and so on. One day he
came to me asking for advice; he was an amateur actor, and
had ambitions towards appearance on the stage in London.
'Good God,' I told him, 'the London theatre is overcrowded.
Stay where you are.' But he persisted, provoking me to a more
vehement warning. 'You'd never get an opening in London.
Overcrowded. STAY WHERE YOU ARE.' His name was Peter
Finch. Then, when Eugene Goossens arrived in Sydney to take
charge of the orchestra and of the Conservatorium, he put on
his opera *Judith*. The principal soprano part was sung by a
young girl whose voice impelled me to write favourably of it.
She came to my flat, encouraged by my notice. She, too, wanted
to go to London. 'Obviously,' I said, 'there's no opera opportunity in Sydney for you, so, if you like, I'll write to Sadler's

Wells and recommend you for a job in the chorus.' 'Oh, but,' she expostulated, 'I don't want chorus work.' 'Really?' I said, 'and what do you want?' 'Oh, I intend to sing in the Met., the Scala and at Covent Garden.' I was speechless momentarily before taking her to task. Her name was Joan Sutherland. I emphatically advised her to 'STAY WHERE YOU ARE'. Finally, —the hat-trick—one Saturday night I was departing from a concert of the Sydney Symphony Orchestra, and one of the oboe players, another young Australian, ran after me. He, too, needed my advice. He was tired of playing in an orchestra; he had set his heart on becoming a conductor. 'Every orchestral player wants to conduct,' I admonished him. 'Keep to your oboe. Wind-players are rare. You'll always be able to get work. Conducting? Great heavens, it's a lifetime's study. STAY WHERE YOU ARE.' His name was Charles Mackerras. If in any doubt about your talents and prospects professionally, come to the Cardus Advice Bureau. Cables and Telegrams: 'Infallible, London.'

Sir Thomas Beecham, as I have told in another place, obtained fair performances from Australian orchestras, which during the early war years were maintained technically single-handed by Sir Bernard Heinze, then Professor of Music at the University of Melbourne. A miracle of tonal transformation happened on the arrival in Sydney of Eugene Ormandy, round about 1944. At once he caused the orchestra there to sound a near relation of his own streamlined orchestra of Philadelphia. Musically, something of depth was occasionally missing, but never, in my experience, have I known a conductor's influence to inspire and direct an assemblage of instrumentalists, some good, some raw and brash, to so high a level of technical excellence. A performance of the Second Symphony of Brahms was polished 'to the nines'—I can describe it in no other adequate words. After this concert, I and my wife saw Ormandy in the artists' room, where the usual gush of compliments was going on, with Ormandy beaming. He asked my wife: 'Did you enjoy it?' And she replied, in her own 'luvly' Lancashire: 'A bit slick, wasn't it?' Ormandy was delighted. 'Never before in an artists' room,' he said, 'have I heard an honest opinion.'

I came to know Ormandy; he was big enough to accommodate my qualified admiration of his conducting. I like him because of his company. He tells a story better than anybody I have known. My favourite of his repertory is of the girl who, with her fiancé, sat every Sunday morning in the Grosser Musikvereinssaal in Vienna. Came the first war, and she sat alone. He was fighting. Then, soon, she sat there in widow's mourning; he had been killed. Then, as the years passed, she grew old, and grey of hair. But every Sunday morning she sat in the same seat, listening to and loving music. She became deaf, dependent on an ear-trumpet. Before the Vienna Philharmonic Orchestra sounded a note, up to her ear would go the trumpet, a look of expectant happiness in her lined, beautiful face. One Sunday morning the programme consisted of Schubert's 'Unfinished' Symphony, and the 'Five Orchestral Pieces' of Schönberg. She seldom read a programme; and nobody had warned her about Schönberg. The light of heaven touched her face as the 'Unfinished' Symphony was played. 'Schön,' she murmured, 'schön.' Then, as the conductor stood in readiness to begin the Schönberg, up went the trumpet again to her ear; trustful and joyous anticipation in her eyes. After a few bars of Schönberg, she withdrew the trumpet from her ear, and blew down it. She was giving music—'die heilige Kunst'—the benefit of the doubt.

Sydney in wartime was a fantasy of self-deception, intended no doubt loyally. At night the city was blacked-out, the edges of the pavements whitened, under a Pacific moon by which a newspaper could be read. Until Singapore fell, the World War might have been a distantly echoing affair from another planet. We accepted a meatless day each week 'for the Cause', and a ration-card allowing us food enough to keep any English or European family well-stored. There were 'under the counter' arrangements for cigarettes. The Sydney Symphony Orchestra began every concert playing all the National Anthems of the Empire and of our allies. Szyman Goldberg, at a violin and piano recital, prefaced his programme by appearing solo, performing 'God Save the King' on his fiddle so devoutly that in my *Herald* notice of his concert I said he made the Anthem sound like the 'Kol Nidrei'. One morning, after the fall of Singapore, a tiny Japanese submarine somehow penetrated Sydney Harbour, where promptly it was sunk. The incident alarmed enough visitants to Sydney from Europe to impel them to take again, and even farther, to flight, to none other than the North Shore of Sydney, some to the Blue Mountains. Thus did I come to occupy my flat in Crick Avenue (No. 35) in King's Cross, a sort of Soho, but a stonethrow from Rushcutter's Bay and Rose Bay. The bays of Sydney are wonderfully beauteous, blue sea and palm trees, with surf refreshing to look at on hot days. But seldom did I leave my flat, my ivory tower, while the world and its far-away peoples raged together. In Crick End I wrote my books—my autobiography, *Ten Composers*, *Second Innings*.

Concerts in bomb-ravaged Europe were rare; as a consequence Sydney and Australia enjoyed temporary musical enrichment. Solomon played Beethoven for us as though sent from heaven. Marvellous was the singing of Marjorie Lawrence, in a wheelchair, a polio victim. In this position of immobility she sang the 'Liebestod' from *Tristan und Isolde* with a vocal art and glorious personal inwardness matched in my experience by no other singer. Marjorie Lawrence is the greatest artist of song and opera produced so far from Australia; in saying so much I do not underrate Sutherland, Melba, and others. I am referring to an *experiencing* artist, a singer of intense yet controlled power of identifying mind and larynx with the creative process.

An odd fact soon forced itself on me in Australia; an inability on the part of Australian music authorities and audiences generally to appreciate home-born talent, until it had been recognised overseas. The cultural climate of Sydney (if I may use so strong a term) was, in my time, a mixture of eager appetite and touchiness to criticism. I have often marvelled how an artist has ever emerged from Australia, especially from Sydney. The average Australian, though often gifted and domestically talented, is ineducable. An inferiority complex causes a psychological condition which is resistant to fuller and non-Australian knowledge, experience and direction. Again—a tougher obstacle to get over in Sydney—the social atmosphere is money material. There is a bank balance snobbishness. A prestige symbol is essential, a Rolls-Royce for preference. The paradox is that the book-buying public in Australia is vastly greater, per head, than it is in Great Britain. The books mostly are bought by women. The average Australian young woman of the war years was on a plane above that of the average male Australian, in intelligence, sensibility and conversation. I made friends of few Australian males. I became involved with at least three Australian girls, each years younger than myself. It was my constant speculation where Australia would veer, as a growing nation—that is, if *ever* the Continent could get rid of provincial prejudices of the kind keeping Melbourne miles apart, not only as the crow flies, from Sydney. As far back as 1936, on my first acquaintance with Sydney, I suggested to one of the professors of history (of some sort) at Sydney University that in less than a couple of decades Australia politically would turn to the United States in a Pacific Confederation, or whatever. The idea was laughed out of hearing. Australia has so far failed to show to the outer world a statesman who is possessed of a more extensive view than that of the next politician. There have been Lyons and Menzies, each larger than Australian political life, maybe, and, naturally enough, not consistently trusted by Australians in the herd.

After Pearl Harbour, spare parts of the United States army descended on Sydney to defend Australia from the Japanese threat to enter by a no means remote doorstep. Sydney abounded with American uniforms, neat, clinical and important. Sydney taxis were commandeered, also Sydney girls, in the absence of their boy friends, away fighting in New Guinea. One afternoon I was playing a gramophone record in my flat, a record of Furtwängler conducting the Prelude to *Tristan und Isolde*. I was playing it to my friend Bernard Heinze, conductor of all the war-time Sydney orchestras, as I have already noted. To demonstrate a Furtwängler tone crescendo, I turned my gramophone on at its loudest, whereat my flat's door was thunderously hammered. I opened it, and an American officer stood on the mat, irate and decorated. 'Shut down that noise, cut it out,' he declaimed. Heinze came forward. 'What's the matter?' he asked. 'That row,' explained the officer, 'stop it, cut it out.'

Heinze faced him severely. 'How dare you come banging at my host's door? Who are you?' 'I happen to be an officer in the United States Army.' 'Oh, are you?' replied Heinze. 'Then let me remind you that you are a guest in this country, so try to behave yourself accordingly.' Then he closed the door. A remark surely to be preserved, worthy of Beecham himself.

I don't think that any music-critic has written in any city with the influence I wreaked in Sydney between 1940 and 1947; not even Korngold in Vienna. I needed to get the values right in the Australian musical scene. War-time was a good period for performers from overseas to exploit a more or less uneducated trustfulness. The once celebrated tenor Georges Thill turned up in Sydney. In my report of his first recital I remarked that 'until last night Georges Thill had been known as a singer in Australia only on the strength of gramophone records [the old seventy-eights]. At this concert he sounded as though in need of a new needle.' An Australian politician's daughter gave a recital in the Sydney Conservatorium; in her programme was Schubert's 'Die Forelle'. I wrote to the effect that she changed it to an Australian schnapper, a toughish fish in home waters. As a consequence of this notice a question was asked in Parliament. Senator Lamp (Labor): 'How much longer are the people of Australia to be pestered with Neville Cardus?' Has any other music-critic's activities been made the occasion of a question in parliament anywhere? No answer was given to the Senator's query; the Prime Minister was stumped. He was, I fancy, Mr. Chiffley, whom I never met; but I sent him, later on, a copy of my autobiography. He wrote thanking me, adding: 'I have read it with much pleasure and have found many interesting statistics in it.'

I became notorious in Sydney. The *Sydney Bulletin* printed a cartoon depicting two street-musicians, one of them saying: 'Look out, Bill, and tune-up. 'Ere's Neville Cardus coming.' It was all tremendous fun. I was the one-eared man in the land of the musically half-deaf. I soon realised that Australians would take criticism if at the same time I could give them a laugh. And I had to accommodate my wit to the Australian broad sense of humorous satire. I daren't be too subtle. At a

Sydney Symphony Concert, Dr. Edgar Bainton conducted the first public performance of a symphony composed entirely by himself, in D minor. He was then Principal of the Sydney Conservatorium of Music. He happened to be a first-rate musician and a very ineffectual conductor. I praised the symphony in my *Sydney Morning Herald* notice, pointing out that though not original, though echoing Elgar and Delius, it was well-written; but, I added, given another performance, a consummation devoutly to be wished, 'if Dr. Bainton again conducted it, maybe he would do fuller justice to the work if and when he was thoroughly acquainted with the score'. Late that night I was rung up in my flat by a sub-editor of the *Herald*. 'Can't understand a paragraph in your notice. You say that Dr. Bainton conducted the first performance of his symphony?' 'Yes,' I replied, 'that is true.' 'Yet you go on to say he'll probably do justice to it at another performance if and when he is thoroughly acquainted with the score. Doesn't make sense. If he composed the symphony, surely he already knows the score. . . .' I could only say: 'God help us, and good night.'

The humour that went down well in Sydney was of the sort contained in a notice like this. A visiting pianist, Paul Schramm ('world-famous', of course, in war-time Sydney) gave concerts in proliferous plenty. 'His concerts,' I wrote, 'are extremely difficult to fix in time and space. In future, on sleepless nights, I shall cease vainly counting sheep going through a gate; I shall count recitals by Schramm, and when I have counted 57, the chances are that I'll be jerked into acute wakefulness, and find myself at a Schramm recital.' On another occasion, a conductor from Perth, Western Australia, flew three thousand miles to take charge of the Sydney orchestra, and of the Fifth Symphony of Beethoven. This concert happened to manifest itself on the evening of the day on which the Melbourne Cup had been run. I wrote my notice of the concert in terms applicable to the English Grand National. '. . . At the first fence the second horn fell; at Becher's Brook the first trumpet and third trombone fell. . . . Result: 1st, Second Flute; 2nd, Double Bassoon; 3rd, Conductor. Also ran, Beethoven. . . .'

On the evening of the day which witnessed the war's end, an

Israeli girl gave a piano recital in the Sydney Town Hall. I imagine that this was the one and only concert happening anywhere in the world on this night of regained, if illusory, peace. The name of the pianist was Pnina Salzman, until then unknown to me and to most folk not resident in Tel-Aviv. Her concert agent telephoned me at my Sydney flat a few days in advance of her recital, inviting me to lunch with her. I declined, pointing out that on principle I never became acquainted with a performer before I had dealt with her strictly in public print. 'If Miss Salzman should be in the mood to meet me after she has read my notice,' I explained to her agent, 'I shall be most happy.' As it turned out, she favourably impressed me at her first of many Sydney concerts; but I gently chided her for trying to cope with the 'Appassionata' Sonata at her early age of twenty-one. I lunched with her on the morning on which my review of her playing had been circulated. After a half-hour of pleasant but gradually communicating talk, she said: 'But you were rather hard on my "Appassionata" Sonata.' I replied: 'Why did you play it at all? You are not ready for such music yet.' 'You must admit,' she responded, 'that I made it sound like the "Waldstein".' Naturally I succumbed. She was—still is—extremely beautiful, with eyes of deep glow, and she has a ripe mouth acquainted with unforced laughter. We became close companions, a happy relationship not at all embarrassing to me as music-critic. She was—and remains—ruthlessly self-critical. Though I instantly admired her beauty and could feel the appeal she put out to men, often consciously, I was not in the slightest attracted to her sexually. We have seldom kissed, merely cheek and cheek. Her beauty for me was something remote. She assured me she was not in Australia in war-time as a refugee. 'I am Jewish, but not from Hitler's Germany. I am from the Old Testament.' I could see her proudly standing in the alien corn. She conveyed a sense of personal independence. Men who fell for her physical attraction were aware of this same withdrawn part of her, I am sure. On the concert platform she would walk to the piano with the carriage of a queen, scarcely recognising the audience. Her agent protested. 'But, Pnina, why do you go on the stage so lofty? You must *smile* at the audience.' 'Why should I smile?' she asked him. 'The audience is not funny.'

At a cocktail party, a member of the Sydney legislature, more Oxford than Balliol itself, approached her in all her sultry splendour and, playing the *gallant*, exclaimed to her breathlessly: 'Ah—Cleopatra!' With a smile of entirely disarming charm, she said to him: 'I am very sorry, but you are not Antony.' She was an artist at the keyboard and away from it. The public at large, and the critics in multitudes, do not infallibly hear repeatedly all the finest natural-born interpretative artists. I have known several lost to renown by marriage or by a preference on the part of the artist to make music privately, or by untimely death. If I were rich enough in money to engage performers for pleasure entirely of my own, Pnina Salzman would be one of the first of all, never mind many of those more prominently loomed in the public eye. I still remember, a quarter of a century after the event, her playing of the 'Études Symphoniques' of Schumann. A curious slip occurred at the attack on the first variation; it was a slip which really told of the pianist's refined sensibility. Trying to get the right darkness of tone, a padded velvet touch in the left hand, Pnina failed to produce *sound at all* on one or two notes. (Heard melodies are sweet and those unheard are sweeter.) There was no break in the rhythm; the impulse was quick and uninterrupted. Best of all, and a rare virtue to be discovered at any time during performances of Schumann's 'Études Symphoniques', the moods and transitions were as though instantaneously presented or, rather, evoked. Pnina Salzman has given recitals in London recently, a mature mother today and ageless, unstaled, and with the most classically antique and regal profile to be seen merely by payment of admission to the Wigmore Hall. The critics of London have praised her playing in a routine way, missing her secret of allurement, too much with eyes not on her but on the score. In Paris the critics are much more susceptible; in fact, they begin with her personal ravishments, and work thence to her preoccupation at the keyboard. I can't understand why, when I first met her, I remained only in the suburbs of her affection. Maybe I was otherwise engaged.

On the Sunday morning of a concert she was to give in the afternoon in the Wigmore Hall, she was rung up by a pianist of international notoriety. 'You are playing the Liszt sonata, Pnina?' 'Yes.' 'But,' persisted the virtuoso, 'but, Pnina, it is very difficult.' '*I* should know,' replied Pnina. End of telephone call. After the recital, he came to her in the artists' room, and admitted he had much liked the way she had played the closing notes of the Liszt sonata, 'the last bars, Pnina, the ferry last'. 'But,' she asked all curiosity, 'didn't you like the little ones in the middle?' Pnina has lived through the Israeli-Arab troubles and suffered. One night when she was in Egypt, she journeyed alone and stood before the Sphinx, alone at midnight; and, she told me: 'I asked the Sphinx three questions.' Adorable, gifted, beautiful, and—very rightly—not a familiar and shared image of the multitudes.

Pnina, though, had to survive much competition from home-cultured Australian girl pianists, almost equally appealing to eyes as to ear—Marjorie Hesse, Joyce Greer, Maureen Jones, Eileen Ralph, Eunice Gardner and Muriel Cohen. The talent for piano playing amongst Australian women constantly astonished me; yet not one truly world-class keyboard artist has so far emerged from the Continent. But, I shall maintain later, at least one certainly should have. None of these girls I have named was professionally an all-time pianist; each was a housewife bringing up children and attending to the physical demands of husbands, sex, food and liquid refreshment, mostly unhelped by servants. The Australian women are, or were, wonderfully versatile, as sweethearts, wives, mothers, mistresses and civilised beings. At cocktail parties the men grouped together in one part of a room, the women in another, conveniently separate. I naturally gravitated to the women. Conversation with the men usually began and ended with sport or money. Maybe I was lucky with my Australian homes and girl friends. In most houses I found that the wife or daughter could sit down on the piano stool and, by means of Chopin, Beethoven and so on, give much pleasure of an accomplished amateur order. Not in London, or any English community, could I come upon so much piano devotion and technical proficiency.

I have often been asked how I could have lived seven years in a city as culturally brash as Sydney. In every large community there is brashness, brashness of different sorts, intellectual as well as provincial brashness. I think of parts or layers of London N.W.8, for example. A paradox of Sydney's social life, as I knew it, was the contrast of middle-aged suburban respectability and a permissiveness which, by years, preceded the 'with it' permissiveness in vogue in London as I write these lines. This Sydney permissiveness was a revolt of young minds and young, superbly healthy bodies against long-since imported stuffiness from England. The girls of Sydney could plunge into bed even as they could plunge into the Pacific surf.

I was staying at a bungalow at one of the beaches, miles from Sydney, where blue sky, blue sea, and great towering surf were, apparently, omnipresent. Myself, a landlubber from Manchester and London, had no use for the enchantments of the Sydney beaches; I dislike the sight of browning, burning, recumbent bodies, male or female. At this bungalow I was secreted in a wing remote from lounge and reception hall. One Sunday I was grappling with the Elgar chapter in my book *Ten Composers* when my hostess came into the room inviting me to take cocktails. 'People are in for drinks from the beach. They know you are here, so please, do come and meet one or two of my friends.' Reluctantly I complied. The lounge was crowded and picturesque, a seaside fashion-plate, a semi-tropical coloured supplement of *Vogue*. One girl approached me, wearing beach costume and a huge circular hat. 'Ah,' I said snobbishly to myself, 'typical Sydney, "Miss Australia".' The girl, trembling a little, asked me: 'Would you recommend the Tausig or the Busoni edition of the Bach Toccata and Fugue in D minor?' She had high cheek-bones, like Milady, a plummish contralto, and a pervasive allure, eyes and the rest of her. In less than a week from this first meeting of her, I was staying in the same bungalow, and she was a guest. One hot midnight I lay reading in bed, protected by gauze from mosquitoes. Suddenly my bedroom door opened; and this lustrous girl entered. 'What are you doing here?' I asked. 'I am coming under that net,' she said, diving under it and into the bed. As I say, as though into the surf.

One Monday noon of fiery Australian sun, as I sat at my writing desk nakedly at work, she telephoned to me saying she thought a baby was on the way, which was disconcerting news for me, seeing that my wife was on the high sea coming to Sydney to join me. My wife and I remained great companions over a period of half a century, but we never shared sexual communication. Nonetheless, another bastard in the Cardus family (the other, myself) could hardly have signified to my wife a warm welcome in war-time to Sydney. I happened at this critical point of my life to have as close friend and father-confessor, Ignaz Friedman, a philosopher as well as a pianist of the Grand Seigneur tradition, stemming from Rosenthal and Paderewski. I told him of my girl friend's anticipation of childbirth. 'Ah, Cardoos,' he pronounced, 'they always say that. I should not vurry. They always say that.' The alarm was a false one; there was no issue. So we, my girl friend and I, resumed essential connections periodically (a good word).

A few months after my wife had settled in a charming flat, a mile from my own, a scurrilous Sydney journalist in a gossip column wrote questioningly: 'I wonder if Mrs. Neville Cardus, wife of the English music-critic and broadcaster, is aware that her husband is frequently seen in the Prince's Restaurant in company of an attractive blond?' My wife at once wrote to the editor of the paper: 'Your gossip columnist appears to be limited, not to say short-sighted, in his muck-raking researches. If he would direct his investigations further, and to the Normandie Restaurant in particular, he would find my husband frequently there with an equally attractive brunette.' In 1947, I returned to London, going back to Sydney in three months; meanwhile girl friend number one had married, and another had left Sydney for Johannesburg, and another had departed to London. It was my routine to take my wife to dinner every Tuesday and Thursday; in fact, it was she herself who insisted on habitual social procedure, with everybody. One morning, not a Tuesday or a Thursday, I rang her asking if she was engaged that evening. 'You know very well,' was her reply, 'that every Monday I go to Betty.' I implored her to put off the engagement. 'I'm at a loose end,' I moaned. She generously accommodated. Next week I once more dislocated her calendar. This time, as we dined, she asked: 'What's the matter? I can't continue putting off my friends.' I explained; this girl friend had married, this one was now in South Africa, the next one in England. 'But,' she asked, 'why don't you take Vera out; she's a very nice girl?' 'Oh,' I said, 'she's alright, but not exactly scintillating.' 'What's wrong with you, Neville,' observed my wife, 'is that you are getting too particular about your girl friends.' All, of course, spoken in downright Lancashire vowels. She was a great spirit and character, born for sisterhood, not marriage. I bow to her, as I write of her here, a year following her death. When she had died, I arranged for a London firm to carry out all the funeral arrangements. The bill of expenses was paid immediately. But a few months later, another bill came to me for the same funeral costs. A reply to the firm stated the date on which the bill had promptly been paid. And yet another similar invoice was posted to me. This time I personally attended to the matter, thus: 'The bill of costs for the funeral of my wife was paid on May 6. You sent me the bill again on June 15. Today, another bill for the same costs has come to me from your excellent establishment. Am I to assume that this latest bill is for Resurrection charges?' My wife would have loved this retort courteous and inquiring. I can hear her saying: 'You ma-ade it all oop.' And perhaps she would have been seventy-five per cent speaking the truth.

King's Cross in Sydney, as I knew it, and lived in it, was the King's Road in London in advance of the King's Road in London's latest swinging time. In King's Cross in Sydney girls were distinguishable from boys at first sight, men from women. Australian girls and women revelled to show their femininity. Australian men and boys asserted their masculinity, and power of lung and larynx. Darlinghurst Road, King's Cross, was a place of many colours. Summer sunshine cast a glamour on the variegated scene; gay dresses, open shirts, well-groomed hair among the girls, and hair chests flaunted by men. Shops displaying the sign 'Delicatessen' occurred at regular spatial intervals, owned as far as I could gather by distant relations of Gustav

Mahler. I introduced the music of Mahler to Australia by the medium of broadcasts, as I have already hinted. From time to time a refugee from Vienna, or thereabouts, a proprietor of a 'Delicatessen', would tell me that he was somehow related to Mahler, a curious form of romantic self-exploitation, far from one's 'Heimat'. There may have been a Freudian reason for it; I couldn't say, and couldn't care less. It amused me, and gave pleasure to the narrator. But long before Hitler, Australia had a sort of enrichment from Germany. Many of the first-class wines of Australia are produced in the vineyards established decades ago by the Burings, the Seppelts, hailing from Hamburg or Düsseldorf or wherever.

I came to know a remarkable old Hamburg emigrant to Sydney, dating from the 1880s. Now he was an octogenarian. Because of doctor's orders he could not dine or taste wine later than mid-afternoon; also he was obliged to take to bed around 8 p.m. So he entertained himself and his friends to lunch in his *gemütlich*, very German-furnished house at Edgecliff, a suburb of Sydney. And he turned day into night, lunch into dinner. Heavy curtains were drawn; the dining-room was secluded with lamp light. The clocks were changed to indicate 8 o'clock in the evening, even as the Australian sun stood poised red-hot at noon. Round the table we sat, the wine glasses and the pictures on the wall and the polished table reflecting the shaded illumination. I am, as I think of this old man's act of illusion, surprised he didn't insist that his guests came in black ties. We would sit there from noon until round about four—or, in the octogenarian's time-calendar, from eight until midnight. Then we departed. He showed us out with a graciousness as aged as himself, waved us away into the blinding prosaic day, our eyes blinking as they adjusted themselves from a conjuration of night. He gave me, as a present, wine-glasses from one of which, he affirmed, Brahms had drunk in his father's Hamburg home; he couldn't remember which glass was the hallowed one, so I vary my genuflexion of palate as I drink from glass to glass today. He played the piano amateurishly but fervently, a Bach Prelude always before lunch—I beg his shade's pardon—before dinner. At the head of the table he would, in a land and epoch alien from his truly own, move my heart as he spoke of the departed spectral past. He was of the family of a Hamburg shipper, a Jew of course. As he sat at his own invocated nocturnal dining-table, the Australian scene outside not only forgotten but temporarily obliterated, I felt acutely the bitter-sweet ache which comes as the mind is stirred by a sense of time dimensionised, so to say; time passing, time gone and time recurrent, time flickering like a kaleidoscope of our consciousness. We have been here before, we are here now; and the enchantment we are now experiencing is on the way out, going, going. The humane cosiness, old portraits on the wall, delicate stems of the wine-glasses, warmth of nature and of flesh and blood, all ready to tingle and flow and mingle, removed from the wear and tear of time, yet surely vanishing. Such an experience crystallises emotions and sensibilities from which we may find an attitude of life and existence, with the mind clarifying opacities of moments not absorbed into one's being and awareness until years after. An old man's self-deception in a continent remote from the Germany of his birth-time; the distant Hitler war a momentary illusion; the years cancelled and all the burden of them fallen for a while from the octogenarian's shoulders; the Australian brazen day transformed to a night in a vanished Hamburg. It is all dream-like to me even as I write of it here. Did it really happen, in Edgecliff, Sydney in June 1941?

Seven years in Australia—seven years is only a brief portion in a mortal existence going beyond the Scriptural tenure. Nonetheless, these seven years in Australia remain in the foreground of the canvas of my life, real, vivid and as though actively present *yet* in my consciousness. I walked on every pavement, day after day, along Castlereagh Street and George Street. In the lovely Botanical Gardens near the harbour I would feed the pigeons at twilight after rain, alone, as the blue mantle of evening began to cover the sky. At such solitary moments I acutely felt isolated from a world, far away, seething in the war's melting pot. It was round about this crucial period of our transient history that unaccountably I broke out into a poetic rash. I had never before tried, or was moved, to write poetry; only once or twice since this strange visitation have I wanted to write poetry at all. The muse of verse was inspired—if I may use so strong a term—by the fall of France. Helplessly distant from the sorrowful centre of events, the news pierced one's loneliness, one's pitiful non-involvement. The watcher from the skies, seeing yet not there! My heart and mind ached for some catharsis. So I wrote as follows: I publish it here without a blush. It may be bad poetry, but it had a cleansing effect on my temperament. I publish it now because of an egoistic pleasure in revisiting my Australian self and situation:

Freedom. *May 29, 1940*

No need now to climb the heights
Until the body aches;
No need now to strain, looking for Pisgah sights
Until the heart breaks.
No need now to whip the fog
Of futile argument,
Trying by stressful logic to prove
That a few of us can remove
The crass things that corrode and clog.
Passion's spent . . .
No need now to climb the heights
Against odds
Seeking—O seeking!—for gods,
The gods are not there;
They are dead, and the summits are bare.
There is nothing left now but Despair,
Peaceful and pitying Despair,
Who sees what she sees,
Says, 'End the vain strife;
I can bring you release.
For I have nothing to give,
Nothing to keep;
No duty to life,
No purpose to live.
But I know of the sleep
That is dreamless and deep.'

I felt much better after getting it out of my system.

The same rash of blank and rhymed prose produced another *cri-de-coeur*. When the air-raids really got to work in London, I knew that a dear girl was there. I sketch her, as I hope to sketch later the crippled Sydney brave spirit, in a few words: she might have walked out of Barrie's *Mary Rose*; she was (still is) Mary Rose plus wit. My anxious fancy needed another catharsis. Hence the herewith unashamedly resurrected lines:

To the Ghost of a Girl of London in War-time
(*Sydney, March 1940*)

And the sun would be warm from the West
Shining from Regent's Park;
Of all London's hours the best
Just before dark.
When the city was touched with a soft calm glow
As if reflected from long ago,
Fragrant and somehow sad.
And a girl and a lad
Laughing; then, hand in hand,
Jump on a bus to the Strand.
And an old man slowly totters by
Due for his club, dinner-jacket, black tie;
And there's a lonely and faded old maid
With her unconcerned dog, and she's half afraid
To cross the street, as the taxis race
From St. John's Wood down Portland Place.

Does your ghost walk alone
Down Portland Place?
Do you search in vain
In all the old corners again
For my face?
Do you run around, even now you are dead,
In panic and dread,
Because I'm not there, not there?
And the sirens wail in the air

And the sky over Regent's Park drops rain
Of hell
While you run pell-mell
Down Portland Place,
From pillar to post
To meet—meet whom? Another ghost?

Peace, my love; no need to race
With fluttering heart down Portland Place.
You are dead.
And the rose is dead.
And I am dead—
A ghost like yourself, wandering in space
Looking for ever for the dear lost face
That once was mine, at my own choice
To touch and kiss—and hear your voice
Laughing and teasing, both face to face
Anywhere;
Between St. John's Wood and Trafalgar Square
Or Oxford Circus and Portland Place.

I became reconciled to my withdrawn condition in the general convulsion. Until Japan ventured into the war, Australia was insulated. As soon as my wife joined me in Sydney—her sister and her sister's husband were killed in an air-raid—I had no personal anxieties concerning what happened in England. ('Mary Rose' had been spirited into Cornwall.) I was, of course, constantly aware that the civilisation which had nurtured all those of my epoch and origin was being destroyed; and I knew that no good could come of it; on the contrary. But there was nothing that I, or anybody else in Australia, could do about it. There was only one job for us—to cultivate our gardens, to tend to Australia's way of life, to aim at enriching it, for, I thought, Australia soon might be needed as another sort of Noah's Ark for the preservation of remaining, if not selected, survivals of European culture. I sat in my top-room flat in Crick Avenue, hours at my desk every day, where in seven years I wrote nearly a million words, not perhaps in the best order but, all the same, words, words, words.

From 10 a.m. until afternoon I remained in my pyjamas. Outside my window the sun seared, or the winter rain descended tropically. I found, by this solitude, some inward truth, a self-knowledge which is difficult to root out in a sophisticated milieu such as persists in, say, London's Hampstead or Fleet Street. At the war's crisis, the world in a hell's melting pot, I steeped my mind for a year in the music of Debussy, relieved, of course, by mundane and social diversions, also by enriching experiences of love and friendship. My memory of this seven year 'Frist'—I was sad when it was 'um'—is kaleidoscopic in movement and sequence. Scenes and people loom and pass and stay on my memory's retina. There was—and still is—Betty. Crippled with polio as a child, she hauled herself about on crutches. A woman friend lived with her, a sister *in excelsis*, by devotion and service. They could not afford a car, and for transport from their house looking upon Watson's Bay, miles from Sydney, they had to use the tram. And this was their technique of travel; when the tram stopped to take Betty aboard some passenger hauled her to a seat, while Maisie, her other half, ran to the tram's rear, there to deposit the wheelchair in which she pushed Betty here and there. On arrival at their destination, a passenger would carry Betty from the tram; and Maisie would race to recover the wheelchair. One day, at the height of the invasion of Sydney by the United States army spare parts, one of the American officers took Betty in his arms, lifting her from her seat. He was about to deposit her on the pavement when, with her own witching smile, she said: 'Excuse me, but I don't stand up.' Nothing, in the history of recorded brave and human speech, has been said wittier and more heart-filling than that. She taught little children piano playing. 'They don't use the pedals also,' she would say. Lately she embraced the Roman Catholic faith, after considerable inward dialectic. Her helpmate didn't like it. 'She's going on,' Betty wrote to me, 'like Oliver Cromwell.' Always a triumphant spirit, so much so that nobody for a moment could take note of her physical disability. Let me leave her at that, portrayed in a cameo which, as far as I am presenting it, enshrines her.

* * * *

13+

In 1936 I first voyaged to Australia, writing about the Test matches when the England team's captain was G. O. Allen. In Sydney we all stayed at the homely Usher's Hotel, now dismantled and inhospitably replaced. On our first night in Sydney I went into the dining-room with William Pollock, correspondent of the *Daily Express*. We had ordered our preludial course, when a violin and piano disturbed my ear.

I cannot abide a restaurant musical accompaniment. I arose from my seat, ready to depart; but Pollock protested: 'We've ordered; and there's nowhere else in Sydney at this time of the night' —(seven o'clock!). I was becoming obdurate; but the violin ceased, and from the piano I heard Schumann's 'Widmung', beautifully floated and fingered. I resumed my seat at the dining-table. Also I sent a special request to the pianist for some Chopin, which was promptly and most musically directed at me personally. I introduced myself to the pianist next day, after I had sent roses to her. This way I came to know Muriel Cohen. When I returned to Australia to write about Beecham for the Keith Murdoch press I travelled at Easter from Melbourne to Sydney by train, a journey involving a midnight change at Albury. As I walked across the platform to the Sydney carriages, Muriel came running after me. She, too, was returning to Sydney and had recognised me immediately. She told me she had recently married—'the handsomest young man in Sydney'. I retorted, 'My God, *you* married? And *you* an artist, a young pianist in a thousand!' She is today a mother of two splendid boys and a beautiful daughter. One of the boys conquered a polio affliction. Her husband is a brilliant, far-reaching man of business. He didn't marry intending that his wife should fly about the earth giving concerts. Muriel brought up her children, attended comprehensively to her husband, as lover and wife, ran a house unaided by servants (you can't get, or keep them, in Sydney) and found time to practise on the piano four hours a day. She is, at the moment, among my favourite pianists. She knows a secret of the keyboard nearly forgotten—how to play on top of it, at the right moment. She has a superb left hand; she plays like a man, a nineteenth-century romantic, with the delicacy of a woman proportionately mingled. Her musical intuitions are uncanny. She recaptures the perfume, the atmosphere of the Debussy Préludes; she can change at will to the different climate and style of Schumann. I count her with Annie Fischer, one of the most satisfying (for myself) of present-day women pianists. She is a rare, nowadays, example of balanced technique and musical intelligence and sensibility. Young students can, at the present time, achieve keyboard dexterities which would astonish, say, Moritz Rosenthal and Paderewski. The piano has been transformed from a means of intimate communication to a medium for putting music over to massed concert audiences. Rosenthal often played, in public, as ...ough to himself. Moreover the technique of the so-called 'romantic' pianists was a servant of aesthetic response, not a master. Muriel years ago played privately to Artur Rubinstein. To prepare for this audition she worked on the Liszt sonata for six months. After he had heard her performance he sat for a moment in deep contemplation, then said: 'Very good, ver-ry good—but not enough wrong notes.' This saying, Muriel maintains, gave her the most enlightening piano lesson of her life. 'I had overstudied the sonata.' She now is fond of saying: 'It doesn't matter much if you hit a few wrong notes so long as you can get the audience to think you could play the right ones easily enough.'

She is so thin physically as to look tall; her cheek-bone structure is fine, her eyes bright as a bird. There is, in fact, something bird-like in her face. She is an inexhaustible, exhausting talker, as Australian in speech and nature as Gracie Fields is Lancastrian. She is, whether she knows it herself or not, a born comedy actress. With an india-rubber face she can suggest a range of characters, high-born, low, middle-class. I love her account of Lady Thing, one of the Committee of an Australian orchestra, who appeared at a dinner party in a gorgeous dress. Muriel asked where she had had it made. 'Oh, my dear, my own exclusive dressmaker in Melbourne'—and Muriel's impersonation was a living sniff of superiority implying that such a garment could not possibly be for the likes of you. But, continues Muriel: 'I rooted it out, took a plane to Melbourne, found the dressmaker, got round her, got the material and had it made up perfectly. At the night of the concert, when I was playing the Schumann, I'm sitting in the artists' room in the interval, all dowdily dressed; and in comes Lady Thing. "Oh," she says, "how nicely and appropriately dressed you are for Schumann" —you know, thinkin' I looked like some German Hausfrau. Then she says: "Well, I must be going back to my seat; good luck my de-arr." Then the conductor comes,—"soon we go on; we begin with the Schumann, Muriel",—but I tell him I want to spend a penny and vanish to the ladies' toilet. And in a jiffy, I change to Lady Thing's glamorous rag. When I get back to the artists' room old Otterloo, the conductor, nearly falls back. "You look vonderful," he says, "but come, we are ready. And bring the music copy; we were not quite together in rehearsal." And I go—phew!—and throw the music into the toilet; and I go on to the platform. And I see Lady Thing's eyes popping out.'

All this is told with marvellously evocative gestures—the 'phew' and cast of hand and arm caused the listener to *see* the departure of the piano score of the Schumann deposited into the toilet. What is more, her performance of the Schumann Concerto, I am convincingly informed, was a rapture of happy rippling notes, and in the Intermezzo, a sheer whisper of enchanting fancy. Muriel, who could not sit back, relax or be still of body or tongue in corporeal life, is changed at the keyboard to an artist reflective, active, introvert and extrovert. 'As I was s'ying, do you follow me?' That is the way her patter goes, 'Orstrylian' and 'refeened' as the occasion demands.

So the kaleidoscope runs on. I see again the dark-haired Viennese in charge of the tobacco kiosk in King's Cross. She preserved cigarettes for me in a period when cigarettes were in short supply. She was another of Hitler's exiled and, by the whimsy of chance, she is typing the manuscript of this book as, page by page, it moves forward in time and backward in remembrance. Her husband, also Viennese, deserves some immortality because of a vastly humorous ambition, unfortunately never fulfilled. He had hoped to be one of the chorus at the Opera in Vienna—just *once* to sing in the chorus. His intent was, one night in *Lohengrin,* when the Herald calls in vain for a knight to come forward to do battle for Elsa von Brabant,—it was his wild dream that he would, in the silence following the Herald's vain summons, dart from the chorus with outstretched arms crying out 'Ich!' It would have made him famous in a night.

The most poignant of the kaleidoscope flashes, though, is of a Christmas Night. After Christmas dinner at Muriel's, I decided to walk the six miles or so back to my flat in King's Cross. Along the New South Head Road I went, past the beauteous bays, the summer moon gleaming on the Pacific waters. I walked with palm trees beside me. In the sky stars shone so clearly that you could see the points, the way a child draws stars. Christmas Night perfumed tropically. Surely this was a Christmas Night closer to the Bethlehem image than the one presented by London's Oxford Street in the slush, rain, chill, with the shops stuffed with mock snow and all the rest of the festive hand-outs. The brashness of Australia? Maybe. But there were islands in the emergent continent, islands of hospitality, friendship, and love, not to forget a hearty togetherness which could be somewhat trying.

RETURN OF THE NATIVE

In June 1947 the native returned to England by flying boat. I was not yet uprooting myself from Australia as a writer; I was going back to London for a refresher, and also because William Collins had that summer taken the risk of publishing my auto-biography. Myself, I regarded it certainly a risk. I had taken years in Sydney to write it. Then, when the manuscript was finished, I acted on advice I have read in something by Somerset Maugham, to the effect that an author after finishing a book should put the manuscript away in a drawer for six months before scrutinising it again. I followed this sage advice. One Monday afternoon, alone in my top-floor flat in Crick Avenue, King's Cross, Sydney, I took the manuscript of my auto-biography out of the drawer of my writing desk, where for six months it had lain in the dusty obscure. I rested it on a table and I read through the handwritten pages. I shall recall the scene and occasion in my last conscious moments of this earthly life.

Outside my flat's window the Australian sun shone pitilessly. In silence I read, on and on. Then I came to a pause, dis-illusioned. The book was not good enough. I picked it up and went out of my flat along a corridor, where an incinerator was installed. I was about to consign the manuscript to the flames, when a voice inside me whispered: 'If the book is no good, let a publisher reject it, not you.'

Next day I gave the manuscript to Collins' manager in Sydney. He sent it joyfully to St. James's Place in London, and

Billy Collins published it. The period was ripe for such a book. The period was ripe for *any* book. Following the war years, everybody was avid for new reading. My autobiography sold in thousands. Had I burnt the manuscript I should today probably be an additional drain on the Welfare State.

London was still, in June 1947, a place of pathetically visible war wounds, dismantled buildings and persistent rationing. There were many pale, lined faces. I was moved to my foundations as I saw the shop-girls going to, or coming away, from work; not one of them, a year or two earlier, could for certain have said she would be alive, or not maimed, this time next week. I felt out of it. My exile in Australia had disqualified me. I could not share the privilege and honour of being one of the immortal islanded multitude that, through darkness and despair and hell, had done its best to salvage, if only temporarily, a civilised way of life. I went to Lord's, my first day in London for ages. Denis Compton was the summer's hero and symbol—symbol of peaceful summer rejuvenation. The London crowds at Lord's, the ground packed at noon, identified their war-weary souls with this image of happy recuperative youth. And they ran his runs with him. At Lord's, on the first day of my revisitation, I went into the Tavern for a drink. I chanced to be carrying in my hand the *Times Literary Supplement*. As I stood at the bar, a Cockney in scarf and cap saw the paper I was holding and put this question to me: 'Excuse me, but are you interested in literature?' The question was, in the circumstances, momentous. I shrugged my shoulders, implying an affirmative. 'Tell me,' proceeded the Cockney, 'what d'yer think of Milton?' The conversation, you will admit, was getting out of hand. 'Why,' I replied, not without coy embarrassment, 'he was a very good poet.' Whereat the Cockney drained his tankard, thumped it down on the counter, and departed from the Tavern, saying to me over his shoulder: 'Milton was a bloody great poet, let me tell you.' At once I was acutely aware I was back in England, back in London. Character and humour of this country had, over seven years, boxed the national psychology—from '*That* means war', uttered by the ancient in the Long Room at Lord's, to this latest memorable statement from one of the once-known as WORKING CLASSES—'Milton was a bloody great poet, let me tell you.'

I returned to London from my sojourn in Australia on the night James Agate died. I had brought a box of cigars for him. In his absence I felt, for a while, that London was now not only war-scarred but deprived of one of its richest humane presences. He emerged from Manchester where, when I was an office-boy for an insurance agent, he went around the shipping houses, canvassing orders for Grey Cloth. During a general election, in a period dominated politically by two parties, Liberals and Conservatives—('either a little Liberal or else a little Conservative')—during this period Agate would do his soliciting, carrying in his pocket a red and blue tie. Arriving at the premises of a firm known as Liberal-supporting, he would retire to the lavatory and put on a red tie. Similarly, before exercising persuasiveness on a known Conservative merchant, he would sport his blue tie. He remained throughout his life an opportunist in his daily intercourse with his friends. For his profession, his art, for the theatre, he was integrity and honesty to the last bone. He would work at a notice with the concentration and care for style and craftsmanship usually regarded as the functional duty and necessity of the creative artist himself. In every one of Agate's notices a memorable sentence used to occur. In Australia, throughout the war, newspapers from London came to us by sea, weeks out of date. Nonetheless, Agate's column in the *Sunday Times*, like Newman's in the same paper, could be read months overdue. Nowadays criticism of theatre and music, even in the weekly journals, is mainly topically descriptive 'of the night'. Notably wit has vanished from criticism. Nobody at present on the job is likely to write as Newman wrote of a prolific but prosaic composer: 'The quartet of Professor Blank struck me as dull and reminiscent. Still, we mustn't be hard on it for, judging from its opus number 259, obviously an early work.' Or J. F. Runciman, in the old *Saturday Review*: 'As for the latest tenor from Bayreuth, singing Siegfried, I was not at all impressed. For the most part of the evening he stood stiffly on the stage, a lay-figure, with his mouth open, until the moment came for him to sing, when he promptly shut it.'

The passing from London of Agate was a harbinger of change on the way, as gusto and unashamed enjoyment of one's personal preferences and prejudices became rarer and rarer. I define Agatism as a relish of one's profession; a pride in it, a pride deliberately cultivated to bring out one's self; a continuous interest in everything likely to bring grist to one's mill. Agate seldom wrote his column without some allusion to, or borrowing from, another writer, usually French. He knew the trick of quotation, how to illumine a passage of his own by a reflected flash of light. He was, of course, a 'square', even thirty years ago. He maintained that any artist, whether poet, composer or painter, should be able to make his meaning clear to an average educated intelligence. He doubted if there was anything in Beethoven which was not reasonably clear to the really intelligent and understanding listener of Beethoven's day. He admitted that 'there must be advancement in the arts, but by advancement I mean not complication'. And he hadn't heard Stockhausen or Messaien! The fact is that compared with, say, the development section of the 'Eroica' Symphony, the most *avant garde* stuff of today (1970) is, related to its period as Beethoven was related to his, pretty naive as far as the exercising of fundamental grey-matter goes. If I were under sentence of death by some lunatic dictator unless, in a year, I could produce a chamber quartet composed in the 'serial' technique, I would not suffer a qualm. In twelve months I could learn the tone-row know-how. My 'serial' quartet might not turn out to be good music, but it would satisfy 'serial' requirements. If the lunatic dictator demanded of me a real tune to go round the world and stay there in the minds of millions for years, a tune as memorable as Lehár's *Merry Widow* waltz, I'd simply throw up my hands and ask the dictator to perform the happy dispatch at once. A study of the evolution of the arts along the ages will convince most readers, not mentally astigmatic, that every conscious *avant garde* movement (advancing in all directions) has quickly run to seed and oblivion. Development means development, deducible continuation, with the twist into a new direction given by a genius who, for all his 'new vision', remains faithful to his medium.

The post-war London of Agate's last years predicted the alteration to come, the engulfment of style and a natural way of life by the onrush of the 'hippie' and the so-called permissive society. Yet, in the 1940s, it was still possible to wear a dinner jacket at the Covent Garden Opera and not be mistaken for the orchestra's first trombone. National Service instructed male teenagers in some discipline and hygiene. Not that I hold the view that the young folk of the 1970s are mainly T.V. by-products, or progeny of Beatles and Rolling Stones. Young people go to first-class concerts in numbers not conceivable before 1939; you will see, any night, young girls sitting alone in London's Festival Hall, listening to Mahler and even to Bruckner, a sight not dreamed of by me, or any middle-aged man, four decades ago.

Youth in the 1970s could put up a show of 'education' not possible in my own period of youth. But it is a *group* intelligence. The Vietnam, Anti-authoritarian Protestants, and most of the other teenage-processionalists, mainly share the same ideas, the same vocabulary—(Involved, Committed, Frustration, Complex, I mean, You know). What is lacking is a personal awareness of things, to the world's way, to ideas, an awareness not prompted by publicity and fashion. The mass medium conditions today. Pavlov's dog everywhere. Doleful songs by Beatles. Yet one of these Beatles has been described by a professional London music-critic as the greatest song-writer since Schubert—at least, so I have been told, though I find it hard to believe.

One of my first impressions of London in the summer of 1947, as I hungrily descended on it as though from a captivity, was of an increase of provincialism. I have told how I was touched by the war-scars, the obviously undernourished girls and youths. I was also touched by the humane togetherness of London's people, in the lump. In the theatre some reflection remained to be seen of the vanished civilisation. A play as obviously literary and charmingly self-conscious as *The Lady's not for Burning*, a theatre-happy audience, with Gielgud and Pamela Brown; masculine *panache* and womanly enchantment in splendid conjunction. Peggy Ashcroft burnt a lovely flickering flame at the Haymarket Theatre in a play adapted from Henry James' *The Heiress*, a flame of beauty, brave and indestructible in the city's bomb-bruised encircling gloom. Edith Evans was a glorious announcement, as Daphne Laureola, of her full-bloom aristocratic flower of comedy; the play was of no consequence; the author was not 'involved' or 'committed', to use the bastardly inane language of those late 1960s. But Edith Evans nightly (and matinées) glorified English life and its inspiring blood and spirit after the descent and resurrection of 1939–1945.

I returned to Sydney in December 1947, only to come again to London in the spring of 1948, voyaging with the Australian cricket team under Bradman's command, his last summer in this country as a player. I had been tempted by W. W. Hadley of the *Sunday Times* to write for the paper about the Test matches. I did not want to write about cricket any more, excepting as an occasional holiday from music. Hadley promised me verbally that the post of principal music critic on the *Sunday Times* would be mine on the retirement of Ernest Newman, a retirement which Hadley imagined would occur coincident with Newman's eightieth birthday. Newman, of course, did not abdicate, so when the 1948 cricket season was ended I was left without serious occupation in music criticism. The *Sunday Times* was prepared to continue paying me a generous salary, but I was remarkably switched to the now defunct *Sunday Chronicle* as a weekly columnist. I suggested to Hadley that, as Newman did not attend concerts regularly, I might be graciously allowed to have some space in the *Sunday Times* every week to deal with events not covered by Newman. I then received a letter from Hadley informing me that Newman had written to him, saying that he had heard of a rumour going around to the effect that he was about to retire and to be replaced by a person 'now engaged on the staff of the *Sunday Times*'. Obviously the 'rumour' had reference to myself, so to quieten anxieties troubling my revered Ernest's mind, I sent in my resignation to Hadley. Next I was requested by Lord Beaverbrook to see him in person, which I dutifully did. He engaged me as music-critic for the *Evening Standard* at a colossal salary, despite that I argued with him that the *Evening Standard* would find my way of writing about music, and my profusion of words every day, rather an embarrassment. So it turned out. My contributions to the *Evening Standard* were generally cut to shreds. I therefore resigned; twice within a year I threw away pounds sterling.

No, I take no moral credit; I was not 'sacrificing' myself for a principle. I was yet again indulging my determination, a lifetime's selfish determination, to enjoy myself. As a youth I was happy to go short of food and bootleather and girls and cigarettes and drink, entirely to comply with my desire to write and live as I wished, for sheer pleasure and dislike of 'work'. I have always defined 'work' as occupation a man would give up at once, were he to inherit a convenient income or fortune. Never since I walked out of an office in 1912 to risk my luck as a professional cricketer (with casual labour in the winter, canvassing for a burial insurance society) have I earned my keep by labour not of my liking. I can honestly affirm, in my eighty-second year, that not once have I written for a moment with my eye on public taste, or out of regard for public demand. The *Guardian*, the *Manchester Guardian*, the *Sydney Morning Herald*, have provided me with enough money to live my life in my own fashion; publishers also have contributed to my indulgences—not excessively; but my need of money has never been for large supplies of it, just enough to give me my necessary good club, interesting women, a decent glass of wine each evening, and a reasonably comfortable place in which to sleep and read and play.

In 1950, praise whatever gods there be, I resumed office as music-critic for the *Guardian*, at much the same salary the paper paid me in 1939. Dustmen, today, are in receipt of an income closely approaching the income paid for my services as music-critic—and I am one of the most aged and most widely-known and respected music-critics in the world. Were I wealthy, I would gladly pay the *Guardian* treble my present salary for the privilege of contributing to its columns. Frankly, since the *Guardian* turned 'national', ceased to be the *Manchester Guardian*, and made its centre of activity in London, critics for the paper have suffered nearly every morning to see their 'copy' cut and even butchered, not because sub-editors have been actuated by malice prepense, but because of, so they say, 'lack of space'. The bulkier newspapers become nowadays, the scarcer the space for writers to stretch themselves in. Also, today, critics at work at night are obliged to conform to a deadline; round about 11 o'clock their copy must be in the *abattoir;* in other words, in the sub-editor's room. In the heyday—the literary heyday—of the *Manchester Guardian,* I was free to write a concert notice at any time between, say, 10 p.m. and 1 a.m. Because of the present prevailing deadline, the rush and the inevitable snap judgment, I decline to write of a new composition. The sad fact is that the critic who is under duress to 'write on the night' is not likely to write well at all. You have only to read the average theatre or concert notice in a morning paper these years to realise that criticism as a form of writing, as an art in itself (I am almost afraid to use this old-fashioned language, even as I write this book for my very own pleasure and company) is pretty defunct, or obsolescent. A few decades ago an anthology of current English writing of quality would have had to accommodate Langford, Newman, Shaw, Richard Capell. Which critic of the 1960s can be said to have a prose style unmistakably his identifiable own? The question is rhetorical; the answer is, there is none. There could be, were the poor scribes given time and space—and if they could take their minds from the music-score and *listen* imaginatively to a concert, submerged of sense, emotion and brain.

To cope with the nightly deadline, I was for a while in torment. I cannot transmit an article by telephone, spelling every name—'S for sugar, H for Harry, O for orange, S for sugar', and so on, right through 'Shostakovich'. Too often I am stuck for an illuminating substitute word—'U for-for-oh, U for unilateral'; then I have to dissect 'unilateral'. A girl friend, with inspiration, solved this problem of transmission of my copy to the *Guardian* office. I ordered a car from Harrods, a limousine with chauffeur. The car arrived at the Royal Festival Hall round about 10.45 p.m. In half an hour my notice was composed in the Festival Hall cafeteria. I then delivered the copy into the charge of the chauffeur, and he and the copy, but not myself, proceeded to Gray's Inn Road, where he deposited the copy into the right hands—with, I hope, a proper show of obeisance. The contemporary habit of cutting critics went to such extremes of abbreviation that my sympathy for the space-harassed sub-editors temporarily dried up. After a performance of the Verdi *Requiem*, conducted by Giulini, I sent a blank page to the *Guardian*—by chauffeur and limousine, of course. I herewith reproduce this nearly blank page:

L .Royal Festival Hall
L Verdi Requiem
L By Neville Cardus
—

Please do not cut.

After a decade of recuperation, following the end of the Hitler war, London and the nation generally assumed a 'new look'; the sociological realists, emanating from comfortable suburban dwellings situated round about Hampstead, had not yet got to work with their investigations into fornication and nudity. Romance still flapped wings everywhere, in the opera house, concert halls and in sport; Callas and Denis Compton, Barbirolli and Kathleen Ferrier, Richard Burton, Elizabeth Taylor and Freddie Trueman, rounding the cape of full personal living. Great Britain was authoritatively informed 'it had never had it so good'; but already there were signs discernible of the dreary reaction to come. The voice of the 'Angry Young Man' was heard in the land. Television took charge in shaping attitudes to existence, manners and daily procedure. A fever of inverted puritanism clouded our cities. Malcolm Muggeridge, temporarily forgetting his assumed role of an unfrocked bishop, recaptured his born wit and stated that the English 'had sex on the brain', which, he added, seemed to him 'a peculiar place, indeed, to have it'. The new Protestants became T.V. essentials, students in procession advertising frustration. Frustration caused by what? Education subsidised by multiferous grants; freedom to express themselves and live reasonably comfortably in a Welfare State which, with British genius for compromise, nicely blended Capitalist economy with Socialism.

I am amused by all this burgeoning of 'frustrated youth', as I remember my own origin as a youth in a Manchester semi-slum, in an epoch knowing nothing of organised State 'Welfare'. You could die if you could not afford a doctor. Landlords ejected a whole family if the rent lapsed into arrears. I and my Manchester companions played cricket on summer evenings on a 'brick croft', dusty where today Bobby Charlton caresses a football as cunningly, as artistically, as Kreisler caressed his violin. As we played our cricket, one bat amongst us, one perishable cork ball, I would see in the distance the tall chimney of the crematorium looming near Didsbury; also in the same perspection, to the left, I would see the sinister lineaments of the Withington workhouse. And I would say to my companions, in good Lancastrian accent: 'Lads, we'll finish up in one of them places or the other.' From the ranks of these Manchester urchins, all sent to work at the school-leaving age of fourteen (the school being a place of mental and aesthetic darkness known as a Board School), from these benighted ranks emerged two professional cricketers (one an England player), a music-critic of international renown, and a *Manchester Guardian* political writer second to none. Where were we educated at all? In the Free Library; and at Charles Rowley's Sunday Institution in the slums of Ancoats. He was a picture dealer, and invited to his lecture hall, and persuaded to address us without fee, such eminent lecturers as Shaw, Chesterton, Belloc, Kropotkin, Ernest Newman.

I was naturally brought up biased against formal education. At my Board School—twopence a week—a dragon of a woman teacher asked me to state the longitude and latitude of Singapore. I honestly told her I didn't know. Why, she inquired severely, didn't you study your geography book? I explained that I wasn't interested, that I didn't intend to earn my living as a sea-captain, or as a sailor; and that if ever, in later life, I should wish to go to Singapore, I should consult a steamship office, where, I was sure, they would know *all* about the latitude and longitude of Singapore. While recounting this episode, which may well convey the impression of a rather cocky school-boy, I assure my readers that I was extremely shy in my early teens. I had been much impressed by a sentence I had read in Samuel Butler, to the effect that nobody should acquire information except in circumstances in which 'he couldn't get on without it'. It is a mistake to clutter the mind with 'knowledge not wanted on voyage'. The problem, of course, arises from the fact that few of us are born with any specific gifts. I have for years regarded the vaster proportion of humanity as the manure necessary to fructify the terrestrial field which produces the Mozarts, the Shakespeares, the Beethovens, the Chopins, and—come to that—the Johann Strausses and Franz Lehárs. Formal education is a dire need in the production of the world's scene-shifters, so to say—the technical staff, the civil servants, doctors, scientists, air pilots, financiers and whatever. No creative mind or temperament can seminally be directed, or nurtured, on what is usually accepted as a formal education, University, Comprehensive, and the rest of it. Even the finest technique, the means of communication in, say, music will count for little if the imaginative seed or germ-plasm was not there in the cradle. My own experience—and it has been experience with a capital E—convinces me that hereditary influence decides mainly the direction anybody takes.

To return to the 'permissiveness' of the 1960s—and in this book I am blissfully at liberty to go here and there and recall my themes, develop them or state them and at once forget them —I am constantly reading, even in the so-called 'quality' newspapers, statements about fornication and nudity which are put forward almost as latter-day revelations. A University don has covered several columns in my own favourite journal more or less discoursing upon nudity and sex as phenomena exhibited openly and publicly for the first time. Probably for our University don fornication and nudity have remained a closed book until forced upon him by the prevalent and pumped-up 'permissiveness'. In my own home, in Summer Place, Rusholme, Manchester seventy years ago, fornication and nudity were phenomena as familiar and as daily manifest as the morning's bowel evacuation, which took place, by the way, in an outdoor shed, done upon a wooden stool, whence blew the wind upward, refreshing one's bottom hygienically. My wonderful Aunt Beatrice (see my autobiography) adorned the oldest profession; so did her sister Ada (my mother), and her sister Jessie. Every evening after work at the ironing-board of an indoor laundry —we 'took in washing'—she would doll herself up glamorously, belladonna in the eyes, rouge on her cheeks, feather boa, silk stockings, petticoats just to be glimpsed. And she would proceed to, or sail down, Manchester's Oxford Street, to 'pick up'. One evening she returned to our tenement crying out: 'My God, Jessie, I've forgotten me French letter.' I was puzzled by this statement, because, child though I was, I knew that my Aunt Beatrice did not understand French.

'Permissiveness'? The word makes me laugh. 'Immorality' in my youth was taken for granted in all strata of society, covered up hypocritically in the Upper Middle Classes under a guise of respectability, even as in these 1970s 'permissiveness is put forward hypocritically to justify uninhibited traffic in pills, contraceptives, Mr. Tynan's quite prim exploration of sex on the stage, and all the rest of it. Immorality, in fact, has been made part and parcel of the time-honoured English capacity of compromise, the knack of making the best of the worlds of virtue and of sin, homage to both—'on the side', so to say.

I saw naked chorus girls in a Manchester pantomime before I had grown out of infants' clothes, short velveteen trousers and sailor collar (on Sundays only). Admittedly, these late Victorian nudes were grouped on the stage to imitate classic sculptures; but they were naked alright. I was not astonished by their exposures; I had since cradle doted on the sight of luscious breasts and rounded thighs. A single silent innuendo, occasioned by an eyebrow and a leer, lifted and projected by George Robey, would today cause a pronouncement of the four-letter word seem as acceptable and respectable as London N.W.8. In a Manchester pantomime Robey deliberately missed his cue for appearance on the stage. Arriving there several seconds late—a long time, measured by audience expectation—he apologised to Maggie Duggan, a Principal Boy of most seemly vulgar magnitude: 'Excuse my unpunctuality, my de-earr, but I have been blocked in the passage'—the syllable 'sage' spoken to rhyme with 'large': thus, 'blocked in the pas-sarge', as though he were flavouring the French language.

*   *   *   *   *

My absence from England for several years, while I lived in Sydney, cut me off from much in London life. I was not a member of the Surrey County C.C for example, so that in 1947, when I went to the Oval to watch the Test match there between England and South Africa, I was obliged to pay at the turnstile and stand in the crowd near the gasometer. During a lunch interval Tom Webster recognised me—Tom Webster, famous sporting cartoonist in his day. He came to me asking if I could get him into the pavilion. 'Oh no, Tom,' I said, 'I'm not a member now—just back from Australia and out of touch.' 'Yes,' he lugubriously replied, 'We've had it, Neville, they've forgotten us.' At this moment a small boy stepped forward and asked Webster for his autograph. Naturally enough, Tom was delighted. 'Of course, sonny,' he said, adding, 'and you should get this gentleman's autograph also. He's a famous cricket writer.' 'Ooh, thank you, sir,' crowed the small boy. And he thrust his autograph book into the hands of Tom, who was just about to sign his name alongside the names of Hutton and Compton when the small boy shouted: 'Oh no, sir, not there!' And he seized the autograph book, turned over page after page hurriedly, and came to the last page, which was headed, written in red ink, 'Miscellaneous'. 'Sign there, please,' requested the small boy. 'You see,' commented Tom philosophically, 'we've had it, Neville. We're "also rans" now. . . .'

In 1947 I was still a member of the National Liberal Club in Whitehall Place. The vast building received a direct hit from a Hitler bomb, demolishing the main staircase. When I re-entered the portal in June 1947, not having been there during the world's years of agony, the hall porter greeted me with: 'Oh, good evening, sir—some letters waiting for you here.' Again, England, my England. Then I met an old septuagenarian friend, who seriously recounted war experiences. At first he was reluctant to go to the club's bomb shelter. 'I was wakened abruptly one morning when the raid started,' he remembered, 'wakened very abruptly by one of the servants, who told me a raid was imminent. I said that I'd prefer to stay in my room; but he insisted, explaining that the shelter was safer, and if anything happened to me, he'd get into trouble for not attending to me, and so on. I agreed to go down to the shelter, so I got out of bed and shaved. . . .' He got out of bed and shaved! While the bombs were actually falling.

Such men then existed; such men probably still exist. We don't know. Apparently, though, they are dying out. I can't quite see many of the 'hippie' generation delighting us, as another vintage M.C.C. member did in the bar of the Long Room at Lord's—own brother, surely, to the Lord's immortal who told me: '*That* means war.' This latest crusted Etonian was grappling with a Lord's sandwich enclosed in cellophane. He twisted it; he tried to tear the plastic covering in vain. Then he turned to me. 'Excuse me, sir,' he said, 'but can you tell me how

I can extricate this . . .?' 'Extricate', the memorable word, to roll over the palate of humour. It is vintage humour that has gone out of our ways of existence in these 1970s. Naturally enough; such humane reactions come from a civilised environment and civilised social usage. As I write these lines, the key words in most serious discussions regarding our ways of existence are 'frustration' and 'involvement'. There's also 'pompous'. I grew up unassisted by any of these words in my vocabulary. Nobody used them habitually. There was, I suppose, plenty to 'frustrate' us half a century ago; we were, I suppose, unable to realise our frustration because nobody on T.V., or in the newspapers, told us about it. We certainly didn't get 'involved'; most active men in 1914 simply went to war when 'Kitchener needed them'. I didn't suspect that C. P. Scott was being 'pompous' when he informed me of my responsibility when, as a young man, he allowed me to edit the back page article of the *Manchester Guardian*, a daily column to which famous writers were glad to contribute signed articles for a payment of five guineas. Joseph Conrad submitted an article for this column. I did not think it was up to our standard. Still, Conrad was Conrad; so I decided to consult Scott. 'If you don't regard it good enough,' he told me, not even looking at the article, 'send it back to Conrad, with the editor's compliments. It is your responsibility, Cardus. You are in charge of the column.' Pompous? I suppose Langford, of all men, would today be thought pompous if he advised a young music-critic, as he advised me, never to write in print anything you would not be prepared to say to a composer or performer face to face.

During the 1960s Flora Robson, an actress who invokes beauty by her presence alone even before her voice makes music, stated publicly that dramatists were no longer writing plays in which women were the focal points. The homosexual had openly revealed himself and was taking the stage's centre. And why not, if the stage must continue to hold up the mirror to nature? My own difficulty in getting into touch with the essential personality of a homosexual is that my own sexual responses are wholly a feminine monopoly. Strangely enough, until I had reached my fortieth year, women scarcely existed for me, except as sisters, a companion-wife, or as aunt. I lived my early *Manchester Guardian* years exclusively with men. In time, by nature's law of compensation, I turned to women finding them, on the whole, much more interesting than men to talk to; and much more pleasant to look at in the lamplight at dinner. I have seldom been seen dining alone with a man these last thirty years. The homosexual is, I find, unusually intelligent, sensitive and witty; and if I am obliged to choose a male for occasional company at all, I prefer a 'homo'. Yet, I confess with shame, I find the homosexual in some way a figure encouraging my sense of the slightly ridiculous, for all my ability to get to his wavelength. One day in my club we were at the bar before lunch, when a beautifully prissy altissimo arrived. He had just, that very morning, bought a harpsichord—'a darling harpsichord'. We were not unanimously interested. Then, somehow, our conversation got on to Bruckner, whereat the young queen again raised his voice: 'But really?' he protested, 'Bruckner? Really? Bruckner? A bore, you know. Dear me, Bruckner? Really?' I could not resist a reprimand. 'There is much difference of opinion extant about Bruckner,' I explained to him. 'In Austria, Bruckner is ranked with Beethoven. In France his music is alien. In this country and the States, there is a growing interest in him. But on one point about Bruckner there is no difference of opinion at all—you can't play him on a harpsichord.'

Frankly I am not interested in other people's sexual proceedings. Richly-sexed men and women take it for granted, and discuss sex no more than they discuss their powers of respiration. My aunt Beatrice never mentioned it. What I feel is wanting in the mental and physical climate of these 1970s is the sense of humour. The present fashion for satire is of an adolescent undergraduate order, with no subtlety or sympathy in it. As I look back over my accumulated years, two important differences in our way of life mark off the 1970s from the 1900s. The Victorians and, come to that, the Edwardians had some positive religious belief. Along with the ability frequently to compromise in matters of principle and behaviour, there was in my youth a recurrent awareness that God existed, or might exist; what was of equal spiritual concern was a suspicion of a Recording Angel somewhere above. The atheists, too, of that period had religion, an ethic to which they submitted; and it was an ethic as demanding on one's moral conscience as any Christian tenet or sanction. Today, in the 'swinging' 1970s, belief in Christianity is not apparently a generally active influence. And—this is the crunch—there is little evidence that present-day non-Christians render allegiance to an ethic of conduct as imperative about self-discipline as the ethic to which we young atheists of the 1900s genuflected, as we attended to the teachings of Huxley, Spencer, John Stuart Mill and Bradlaugh, each of these eminent Victorians relegated now to the pompous obscure.

I have, since boyhood, been unsuccessful in my efforts to—in the Church's term—find God, though, God knows, I have tried. It's high time I made up my mind on this point; though, personally, as I think none the worse of anybody who hasn't found *me*, I fancy the good Lord, if good Lord there be, will not cast me out because of a flaw in my spiritual radar preventing me from getting into touch with Him. I am as impatient with the positive atheism of, say a Bertrand Russell, as I am with the positive God-knowledge which the clergy sincerely—God knows—thinks it possesses and shares. I console myself, in my moments of troublous religious doubt, by imagining some such scene and conversation as this, at a mortal's moment of the Last Judgment:

Scene: Heaven.   Time: Eternity.
(God weighing in the balance of his hand an archbishop)

Chorus of Archangels
'Die Sonne tönt nach alter Weise' . . . etc.

God: Have you always believed in me?
Archbishop: Always, O Lord.
God: You have never doubted my Existence?
Archbishop: Never.
God: You have not needed to wrestle with your faith?
Archbishop: I have always conquered doubt.
God: I was not a Mystery insoluble by mortal means of investigation?

Archbishop: I was given the Light wherewith to find you by my Church.

God: There are many Churches, many creeds. You must serve for a while in my Purgatory, so that you may be cleansed of too much faith. Next please.

      (*Enter myself, into His hands.*)

God: Have you always believed in me?

Myself: I have tried. Metaphysics has taught me to distrust man's ability to cope with conceptions not rationally ordered. I have questioned Kant and Descartes and Saint Francis. I have sought you down the labyrinthine ways. I have argued with my atheism that the creation of a Mozart is not reasonably explicable by any theory of physical or Darwinian evolution. I have always had an uneasy suspicion that, after all, I should hear the Last Trump one day and find myself rudely awakened from my grave, still in my winding-sheet, saying: 'Could you believe it? True, after all; we've been deceived by those damned cocksure rationalists, Joseph McCabe and J. M. Robertson!'

God: So I have remained Incomprehensible to you, even Unlikely?

Myself: Yes. Incomprehensible for sure.

God: Pass on. Your place momentarily in my Establishment will be with Voltaire, Shaw, Elgar and the Holy Ghost. Next candidate, please, Muggeridge— I beg your pardon, Saint Malcolm . . .

Continuing pompously I herewith thank whatever gods there be for a sense of humour, for wit, receptivity to the radiations of a human personality, whether emanating from Shaw, Langford, Newman, Kathleen Ferrier, Schnabel; or Denis Compton, Frank Woolley or Bradman; and most gratefully of all I acknowledge the gift given me to feel the exquisite ache of heart and consciousness at the passing of time as it goes its way, oblivious of us, so that the bloom on the hours is always vanishing, receding with the kiss of the beloved, the beloved herself and her allurement, the eventful day, hour by hour, all of our pulsations to scene and to every visitation to our capacity for imaginative and delighted participation in the 'day's diet of events and sounds'—all of it will not stay; it is blissfully here, poised in our awareness as though for ever; but it goes, and there is only memory left to echo and reflect in the procession of our periods of grace. Without this response to time's magical vanishings, a man, or a woman, has gone through this world spiritually half-deaf or myopic. So let me praise and remember and bow in thankfulness to Langford, to Haslam Mills, and to my women—Matthew, Mark, Luke and John, blessed the bed they lay upon.

*   *   *   *

In 1931, alone in Salzburg, I wandered one morning near the Mozarteum and read, on a poster, that a lecture was about to begin within on Strauss's *Die Frau ohne Schatten*, by a Mitia Mayer-Lismann. As the opera was to be performed the evening of this same day at the Festspielhaus, I paid the fee of admission and listened with admiration to a greying, distinguished woman, who played examples from the opera's score at the piano and explained the involved libretto with charming lucidity, also giving the right point to her music quotations. So satisfied was I with the lecture that I met the lecturer and thanked her; moreover, I wrote in praise of her work in a message to the *Manchester Guardian*. I saw no more of her for years. 'Alles endet was verstehet!'

Then at the Edinburgh Festival in 1948 I was greeted in the Festival Club one evening. The face was somewhat familiar, a white-haired lady of distinction, Mitia Mayer-Lismann—ah yes, Salzburg lost ages ago! A fortnight later I went to hear Furtwängler and the Berlin Philharmonic Orchestra in the Albert Hall; and during an interval I ran into Mitia Mayer-Lismann again, this time with her daughter, Else, tall, terrific eyes, driven in her mid-twenties from her home in Frankfurt by the Nazis, Jewish, of course. She mastered English and the English way of life. She created in a schoolroom in Kensington an Opera Workshop, created it on a shoestring. It is one of the

finest schools of its kind anywhere, inspired by a woman of so
much radiating influence that talent is not an adequate word
by which I can describe her. In the Purcell Room she and her
students gave scenes from *Die Zauberflöte*; the programme was
described as 'Workshop in Action'. Myself, I should have described the occasion as 'Mozart in Action'. Seldom have I been
brought as closely to the heart and mind of Mozart as by Else
Mayer-Lismann and her company on December 14, 1969. The
opera's first performance ever was probably informed by the
simple, unselfconscious potency of this Purcell Room manifestation. I have always believed that *Die Zauberflöte* must not be
'presented' but evoked, as a visitation to us, scarcely aware of
its power, its miraculous mingling of sublimity and fairy-tale.
We should receive *Die Zauberflöte* as *grace*; and it is difficult to
do that if sophisticated performers are diverting our attention
to their rare but inevitably egoistic presences.

On the stage Mayer-Lismann, adorned in long black gown,
might well have been a priestess out of Sarastro's temple—but
a priestess of wit, charm, as well as of encompassing personal
control. When the Priest appeared before the student playing
Tamino, saying: 'Wo willst du, kühner Fremdling, hin?' and
the student showed little interest, she exclaimed to him: 'Why
do you not look surprised? Were you expecting him?' She
moved as a sort of handsome woman medium through whose
mind, nature, eyes, mouth and hand Mozart got into communication with us. The students in their several parts were excellent
enough; but each was under, I could well believe, Else Mayer-
Lismann's hypnotic influence. Only a black curtain served as
the background for this re-creation of *Die Zauberflöte* with the
simplest necessary 'properties'—spears, Papageno's bells and so
on. Mayer-Lismann told the audience that there would be no
'producer' actively engaged during the evening's proceedings,
which was for myself a relief. I do not suggest that performances
in opera houses proper should dispense with scenery or 'production' altogether, but I *do* maintain that in recent years the
producer in opera has been a distracting nuisance, a barrier, a
'no man's land', standing or gyrating between us and the music.
Every opera producer should get to work strictly through the

music. At Bayreuth, in Wieland Wagner's period, I saw a 'production' of *Tristan und Isolde*. If I had been accompanied at this performance by somebody utterly ignorant of *Tristan und Isolde* I would have wagered a hundred to one against the likelihood that he could have rightly answered a question put to him as the curtain rose: 'Where are we?' He could not, either by inductive or deductive logic, have arrived at the conclusion that the first act was set on a ship at sea. It was after this 'production' of *Tristan* that I asked Wieland Wagner if he could remember, more or less approximately, in which year he became a confirmed anti-Wagnerite. He received the inquiry with a wry laughter.

Mayer-Lismann and her work is, as I write, known to a comparatively few discerning people. Today it is publicity and T.V. that establish value of all sorts, political, social, moral and revelatory Christian. I rank Mayer-Lismann, both as individual personality and as inspiring leader, rare among the vital spirits I have known in my life. As I have already hinted, the best often is not universally perceived.

*　　*　　*　　*　　*

I take no personal credit from the fact that I emerged from a generally illiterate home (although my Aunt Beatrice had worldly wisdom and some talent at imitation of 'style', as she saw it in the theatre and learned it by her good taste to procure men of some social standing. And the same I can say of my mother). I have always trusted to my instincts and to my belief that a man can do well only the things he wants to do and is prepared to go to the wall, to starve, to get them. I pushed a handcart around the streets of Manchester at the age of sixteen. I knocked at the door in slums at the age of twenty trying to sell burial insurance policies. I would not 'work' for my living; that is to say I would not commit myself to any apprenticeship to a trade—according to the custom which directed the destinies of youths of the 'lower' classes of the late 1900s. I did not smoke until I was past my twenty-first year. Girls didn't exist for me. I did not sleep with a woman until near middle age. I was unacquainted with alcoholic drink until my twenty-sixth year. I and my boy friends never thought of sex as such. I satisfied casual propensities second-hand from books, theatre and music. I adored Beatrix Esmond, adored Tess, got sensuously intoxicated with Tristan, raped, in imagination, Carmen. It was a good preparation of actual physical and rich-blooded and rich-minded pleasure and experiences to come. Self-educated? —no, I was directed by forces born within me. As I say, I indulged these forces, selfishly. So that, if heaven awaits me, and if I shall, after all, go before the Judgment Seat, I shall say, bowing humbly and thankfully before the Presence: 'I have nothing to declare except the genius you, O Lord, gave unto me in my cradle.'

It is as well that a man, whatever his calling, profession or vocation, should periodically overhaul his catechism, look to his tastes, standards whereby he values. Especially should he submit himself to drastic intellectual and aesthetic examination if he is engaged in any sort of public critical writing. He should beware of becoming predictable by his readers. Few critics escape such a fate of habit and inelastic mental and emotional response. I could name one or two music-critics, much to be respected on the whole, of whom it could be said that for decades their reactions, mental and temperamental, to, say, Stravinsky and Britten have not changed a jot; we have been free to forestall any opinion by these critics of a new work by either Stravinsky or Britten; we have known before the event that these critics would find no important basic fault; we have known that these critics are as much conditioned to Stravinsky and Britten as Pavlov's dogs. Likewise we have been able to wager six to one on an unresponsive reaction of these same critics to Mahler—indeed to any late nineteenth-century 'Romantic'.

It is, of course, a vain aspiration on any man's part to deny, or seek to evade, the personal equation. At all stages of his development his mind can hold only so much. I doubt if the accumulation of years brings wisdom. I confess that I have failed, after much endeavour, to discover the touchstone needed to get at the heart of 'objective truth'.

For my own part, the longer I live the more I am compelled by honesty to rely on personal taste. The wider my studies, the deeper my experience, the stronger and more insistent my temperament controls become, and the less interest I can work up in productions which do not engage my own hard-acquired means of critical assessment. My intelligence, my cultural training, assure me that so-and-so's symphony is excellent in its technical and structural make-up, but I cannot, because of a taste (not narrow!) cultivated in a certain way, another climate than so-and-so's—I cannot, in a word, find his wave-length. By critical awareness, by understanding of technique and what-have-you, I can praise a composition to which my temperament does not respond. Sir Thomas Beecham would not even make this compromise; if he could not 'like' a work, he would have none of it. Bach even. I constantly argued with him: 'I also, Sir Thomas, am often allergic to Bach. But my acquaintance with music, the way it is put together, my critical standards, convince me that Bach was a great composer. It is my temperament, my emotional pressures, that won't join in.' 'Bach is a period phenomenon. A bore,' Beecham would retaliate. 'You can hear bars ahead what is coming. Too much counterpoint. And, what is worse, Protestant counterpoint.' Incorrigible.

I have never, as man or critic, been vain enough to suppose I could see the object as it is in itself. I have had trouble enough searching out truth as I have had instincts towards it in myself. I have always, since I have developed as a thinking being, been diffident about positively marking out subjective thought and reactions from objective reality, whatever that may be. For me, as for Bishop Berkeley, *esse* is *percipi*; at any rate, as regards sensations or messages received from the arts. No two healthily organised humans disagree about the shape, value and identity of, say, a table or a great racehorse; nonetheless, most of us fail inexplicably to find a wave-length taking us to all manner of creative visitations. Only the auctioneer, as Oscar Wilde pointed out, is free to appreciate *all* schools of art. I have perpetually, in my writing, been careful not to ignore my blind spots. As I say, my knowledge and understanding of an artist's technique and of his place in the climate of his period assure me of his standing and importance; yet he may, because of some short-circuiting in my receiving-set of sensibility, fail to kindle in me a full aesthetic participation. I confess my ability to go through my musical life *unaccompanied* by Bach; still, as a critic with a culture, I should be the first to call a fool anybody denying Bach's genius. The difference between the trained and the layman critic is, briefly, this: the trained critic can say 'this music bores me, though my intelligence and training assure me it is the work of genius'. The layman says 'this music bores me, so I conclude it is not much good'.

I have never written with a public in mind; indeed, I have never written with an editor in mind. I have written for myself, to get to the bottom of myself and, mainly, to enjoy myself. Writing has been my liquor, my pill, my drug, my aphrodisiac. Certainly I have never set out to educate anybody, or to tell a performer technically what he should do. If, say, Menuhin plays out of tune—let us constantly bear this fact in mind—there is a reason for it, explainable by a psychological reaction in himself as artist. I am qualified as critic to point out the technical limitations of a young musician, not to teach him the technical know-how. I have, throughout my professional life, been concerned only with responses to music, to cricket, to theatre, to books, to anything or anybody—responses of a man who in his own way has also tried to be an artist, an artist in the reception of, as I call them, visitations of delight, intimations of the range of human capacity to transcend dreariness, the un-beautiful and the routine. And the greatest of these visitations to me have come in the guise of beauty, humour and wit, captured for all time in a composition or book or picture, or given to me by the gods only momentarily in the mortal, sadly perishable shape of woman, fiddler, cricketer, actor or, in company, of a good talker and listener.

It is pretty certain, though, that the day will come to all of us, sooner or later, when responses of the aesthetic antennae will get unaccommodating; after a long lifetime of harvesting, the mind might easily become so fully stored that there is little room left. And there is no fool as foolish as the old fool who runs about presuming to be as young and 'with it' as the next teen-ager. Wisdom is content to accept the fact that a man's taste and standards of comparison have been nurtured and developed in a certain period and soil. He cannot extend the base of his pyramid of aesthetic awareness. If he is sensible he will consolidate the gains of his impressionable years. Vintage comes from some lengthy cellarage.

I am now regarded, as a critic, as a reactionary 'square'. I am amused to remember that, decades ago, I was fighting the unending fight for 'modernity'. None of the present-day young lions is raging so furiously about Stockhausen and Messaien and Schönberg as the young lions of yesteryear raged about Stravinsky and Strauss—yes, even about Strauss, whose *Elektra* was, in its beginning, a nuclear bomb of 'progressive' musical energy. We can see in these *avant garde* 1970s that Strauss was always a traditionist. Why could this fact about him not be seen clearly half a century ago? We must philosophically accept the truth that in every period the critical vision is bound to be focused in a certain way; it can achieve some clarity and definition, confined by subjective personal limitations of appreciation, only when the object to be perceived is situated or presented to it at a certain point in time and space. At a rehearsal of one of Schönberg's most esoteric works, one of the woodwind lost his way in the score. After the rehearsal he apologised to Schönberg for his error; but Schönberg apparently had listened with satisfaction. 'Surely, Meister,' said the woodwind player, boldly, 'surely, you don't mean to say that even *you* aren't aware when your music is being performed all wrong?' 'No,' Schönberg replied, thoughtfully, 'no, not always. But my grandchildren will be.'

H31 920 319 3